HERE COMES THE SUN

Andy McCarthy is a storyteller and passionate lover of life. He thrives on creating connections with others and wants to make an impact wherever he goes. Andy met his soulmate, Kelly, as a nineteen-year-old and they spent several years living abroad, backpacking through more than seventy countries, gathering life experiences and saying yes to anything that promised an adventure. Upon returning to Australia in their late twenties, Andy and Kelly moved to a tiny village in the hills above the Latrobe Valley to start a business and raise a family, immersing themselves in the local community while raising three energetic boys. Despite the pressures of being a global changemaker in the energy space, Andy always makes time to travel across Gippsland to coach, umpire and cheer on his boys' sporting endeavours.

PRAISE FOR *HERE COMES THE SUN*

'An inspirational story; a must-read for any aspiring leader.'
Tony Wheeler AO, founder, Lonely Planet Guidebooks

'Andy's powerful and inspiring account is a ray of hope. His fascinating journey from a troubled youth to becoming a leader in Australia's energy transition – the highs and lows told with honesty and vulnerability – will provide inspiration to anyone working to change the world for the better. We need people with courage, vision and a commitment to their communities to guide Australia through these times – and Andy has these in spades.'
Simon Holmes à Court, convenor, Climate 200

'Andy's story is a compelling read for everyone. As an entrepreneur who can relate to many of his highs and lows, I found Andy's journey both inspiring and enlightening – a true testament to the power of resilience and innovation in driving positive change.'
Adrian Critchlow, co-founder, Booking.com and founder,
Australian Solar Group

'There is nowhere more exhilarating than to be at the forefront of the clean energy revolution. Andy has had a tremendous impact on the Australian energy landscape over the years, inspiring those around him and developing the leaders of tomorrow. A thrilling story revealing the passion, authenticity and care of a true leader.'

Kane Thornton, chief executive, Clean Energy Council

'Personal. Compelling. Insightful. A captivating account of an incredible success story, which provides inspiration for those of us across the globe who have admired Andy's journey.'

Conall Bolger, president, Irish Solar Energy Association

'Not many stories will have such a practical impact in your life. *Here Comes the Sun* is a must-read to realise that anything is possible.'

Gus Balbontin, director, investor, advisor, explorer

'A heartfelt and honest account from the forefront of Australia's energy transition, from one of the solar industry's most inspiring pioneers.'

Stan Krpan PSM FAICD, chief executive officer, Solar Victoria

'Andy's story encapsulates a critical lesson for the transition to renewable energy: it can be good for consumers, good for the planet and good for business. An honest look at the highs and lows of a good and admirable person, trying and succeeding at making a real difference.'

Lily D'Ambrosio, Victorian energy minister

'Andy McCarthy has forged an incredible legacy in Gippsland, and this book captures his richly informed journey in a powerful and authentic way. Andy's unwavering belief in our region's future and ability to bring others along with him have been inspiring and infectious. Our future is considerably brighter for Andy's leadership, and I am so pleased that he has documented his story, and explored his big-hearted lived experience and personal challenges, for others to take learnings and inspiration from.'

Kellie O'Callaghan, former mayor, Latrobe City Council

'This book is more than a biography; it is a beacon of hope and a call to action. Andy's story reminds us that with passion and determination we can overcome any obstacle and create a brighter future.'

Adrian Noronho, CEO and chairman, Schletter North America

HERE COMES THE SUN

ANDY McCARTHY

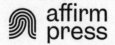

affirm
press

affirm
press

First published by Affirm Press in 2024
Bunurong/Boon Wurrung Country
28 Thistlethwaite Street
South Melbourne VIC 3205
affirmpress.com.au

Affirm Press is located on the unceded land of the Bunurong/Boon Wurrung peoples of
the Kulin Nation. Affirm Press pays respect to their Elders past and present.

10 9 8 7 6 5 4 3 2 1

 A catalogue record for this
book is available from the
National Library of Australia

ISBN: 9781923046337 (paperback)

Cover design by Alex Ross © Affirm Press
Typeset in Garamond Premier Pro by J&M Typesetting
Proudly printed in Australia by Opus Group

Contents

Prologue

It started with a twitch in my left hand. Faint at first, then noticeable and uncontrollable. Then my right hand followed suit. I felt my heartbeat start to increase. My throat became dry, and my chest started to tighten.

I jumped out of bed, paced an anxious lap of the room and sat back down. It was getting worse.

I moved to the spare bedroom and dropped to my hands and knees in the middle of the room. Sweat started pouring down my eyebrows, nose and chin, creating a pool on the hardwood floor. My whole body was convulsing violently at this point, and my chest had contracted so tightly that the pain was becoming unbearable.

I thought I was having a heart attack.

Mercifully, the chest pain started to ease. Rather than call an ambulance, I threw on my sneakers, headed out the front door in the middle of the night and pounded the streets and laneways of

Barcelona at maximum intensity. It was 2am, still 30 degrees, and I had no idea where I was, or how long I would be out there for. I channelled my inner Forrest Gump and just ran.

When I couldn't physically run any longer, I staggered back in the door. My heart was beating so fast that it felt like it was about to burst out of my chest. I set the ceiling fan to full speed, stumbled into bed and lay there shaking uncontrollably for what seemed like an eternity. Eventually, my body gave up and I passed out from utter exhaustion.

When I woke up, I was terrified and confused at what I had experienced.

After years of hard work and perseverance, and more than an ounce of good fortune, I'd just sold the business I had started from scratch to an iconic Australian brand. It was a life-changing moment, a dream come true.

It wasn't supposed to feel like this ...

Chapter 1

Bumpy Beginnings

If you'd met me as a sixteen-year-old, you wouldn't have been very impressed. And if I'd told you that I would end up in the news, you'd be forgiven for assuming that it would be for all the wrong reasons.

The formative years of my childhood were far from ideal, attending school in a gritty and disadvantaged area in the northern suburbs of Geelong. My memories of the bus trip to school are filled with images of broken windows on houses, cars lifted up on blocks in the front yard and young parents smoking at the doorstep while toddlers ran around the yard in their nappies. Passing through the suburbs of Corio and Norlane twenty-five years later was an eye-opening experience. The area has been cleaned up somewhat, but the sense of struggle and entrenched disadvantage is still evident.

I was born to a father of Irish descent and a migrant mother who came out from Holland as a three-year-old for a new life in

Australia with her parents and six siblings. Her dad (my grandpa, who I referred to in the Dutch parlance of 'Opa') was ushered from the plane and sent off to work in a factory in regional Victoria for many months, while Mum and the rest of the family were escorted hundreds of kilometres away to the Bonegilla migrant camp on the Albury–Wodonga state border. As someone who struggles to deal with my three exuberant children at times, I can't imagine how my 'Oma' (Grandma) managed to raise seven kids by herself for so long, with no grasp of the English language and without a driver's licence to get around. Oma was an absolute powerhouse, and it's clear where my mum gets her incredible sense of selflessness and desire to care for people from.

Mum was eighteen when she met Dad (who was six years her senior), and they decided to get married after only six months together. With a significant age difference and a very brief courting period, the response from Mum's family was unsurprisingly hostile, so they decided to elope. Dad was frozen out of the extended family for years, but being a persistent type, he kept turning up to family events despite not being welcome. One day, at a family birthday, after years of not speaking to him, Opa silently extended his hand and offered my dad a glass of port. The war was over. He must have decided that Dad wasn't going anywhere so he might as well get used to him.

We moved around a lot for Dad's work. He joined the Air Force as a radio technician, and this took him to far-flung places like Tom Price, which regularly features in the list of hottest towns in Australia. A forecast above 40 degrees Celsius is nothing newsworthy in Tom

Price; in fact, it's nearly the average temperature for the entire month of January!

From as far back as I can remember, I was always looking for trouble. My parents and siblings bore the brunt of this destructive mission. At fourteen, I was belatedly diagnosed with attention deficit hyperactivity disorder (ADHD), but back in the 1990s no one really thought of it as an illness. Mum was my strongest advocate and she did everything she could to support me and keep me on track. She backed me even when my behaviour was inexcusable and everyone had given up on me (including myself). I still remember how much it devastated her when she would explain at yet another meeting with a teacher that ADHD was driving my behaviour, and they would scoff, 'There's no such thing as ADHD – it's just an excuse for bad kids and bad parents.'

My report cards from each grade of primary school looked like they had been copied and pasted, although the language became stronger with each passing year as I became more of a thorn in the side of my teachers.

'Oral and comprehension skills are well developed.'

'Speaks clearly and with confidence when addressing his classmates.'

'Spelling, punctuation and grammar skills are excellent.'

'Struggles to maintain concentration.'

'Regularly disrupts others.'

'Classroom and schoolyard behaviour is unacceptable.'

My final report in Grade 6 from Mr Farrell concluded with:

'Andrew's academic standard is very high. General behaviour is well short of acceptable level. Good luck, Andrew.' I can almost hear the exasperated tone as he wrote that last line. I'm sure he would have been tempted to add: 'You're going to need it.'

After an increasingly turbulent primary school existence, I was bundled into the only secondary school that would take me, a 'place of last resort' called Flinders Peak Secondary College in Corio. The physical location of the school seemed fitting. The Herd's abattoir was located less than 500 metres away, and when the wind blew from the west, the choking fumes from the slaughtering process added a literal bad smell to the energetic stench of the school. The teachers and principals tried their best, but they were no match for the motley crew of troublemakers that had been inflicted upon them.

Recently, I googled 'Flinders Peak SC', and the first result that came up was an article saying the school had been closed after years of neglect and the state refused to refurbish it. The images were of a faded sign on the dilapidated gym, with car skid marks on the grass in the foreground, and a pile of smashed TVs and school rubble. I believe it was turned into a drug and alcohol rehab facility in 2019, which, sadly, feels like a logical progression.

During my time there, I was bullied by the popular kids, physically and mentally beaten into submission over three harrowing years. It became so bad that I would pause at the end of each period and look both ways before leaving the classroom. But they would always find me at some stage. I can still feel my blood run cold at the sound of their feet shuffling into the locker room behind me as I grabbed my books between classes. I can remember them smashing my head against the locker door and kicking me while I was on the ground, the crowd cheering them on.

Shamefully, I responded in turn by bullying the few battlers that I deemed to be beneath me in the 'pecking order', taking out my frustrations by making their lives a misery. It provided a fleeting sense of self-confidence, although I was oblivious to the awful irony of this.

The teachers had no control over the classroom or the schoolyard, with the students whipping each other into a frenzy and making it impossible to regain control once things started to escalate. I still remember a young maths teacher cowering in the corner, shaking and sobbing, as the usual suspects terrorised her and the other students. It was utter chaos, and I was absolutely swept up in it.

I always completed my work early in class, but the school structure at Flinders Peak wasn't exactly set up for bespoke learning and development plans. The teachers would tell me to sit there and occupy myself while everyone else completed their work. Not surprisingly, I chose to spend this free time distracting others, causing trouble for the teacher or my classmates and generally making a nuisance of myself.

After years of struggling to concentrate, a doctor prescribed Ritalin to help smooth out the peaks and troughs of my ADHD. It certainly did that, but it also turned me into a complete zombie, and had the unfortunate side effect of making me throw up every day for several months. So we chose the lesser of two evils, and I went back to being a jerk (albeit an unmedicated jerk).

I was drawn to the chaos breaking out around me, spending more of my lunchtimes in the principal's office than I did in the schoolyard. Our school had a coloured card system: a white card was issued for minor indiscretions (valid for a week), a yellow card for transgressing while on a white card, then orange, then the final indignity of a red card. Each of the (frequent) red cards earned me a two-day suspension, followed by a week of lunchtimes in Mr Logan's office. The silver lining is that it probably saved me from a fair share of beatings in the locker room.

At home, my destructive behaviour caused a great deal of pain and suffering for my family. Mum and I were very close and she advocated for me far more often than I deserved. Dad reacted as you would expect from a parent at their wit's end, which gave me some sort of perverse pleasure. It's quite remarkable that Dad and I have a functioning and friendly relationship now, as back in those days, our relationship drifted between cold indifference and mutual hatred. At this point in my life, I even hated myself and what I had become, but my response was to double-down and act out even more, sending me down the slippery slope to a dark place. Reflecting on who I was at this point in my life fills me with a fair amount of shame, and it's uncomfortable to write about. But I want this to be an honest and raw account of my journey, which means including the parts I am not proud of.

There was nothing happening in my life to excuse this bad decision-making. In a financial sense, we were merely existing, with few of life's luxuries but keeping the bills paid. I came from a stable home with two younger sisters, and despite the ugly relationship with Dad over those turbulent years, I'd been dealt a fairly solid hand in life. Not that I realised how good things were, and I spent several years either being shunted around to family and friends to live with them for a while or attempting to run away from home. I remember befriending a bloke up the road, and after one particularly heated run-in with Mum and Dad, I arrived at his door with a backpack full of clothes and said I wanted to stay there for a while. He took a deep breath and said, 'Mate, I don't think you realise how good you have it.' He sent me back home.

But through all the chaos of my teenage years, there was one constant that eventually became my saving grace.

I was *obsessed* with making a buck.

With very little going for me, and drifting between groups with no sense of belonging, I wanted all the latest and greatest possessions in life to manufacture a sense of self-confidence. The latest sneakers and clothes (Reebok Pumps and Adidas snap pants!), basketball cards, video consoles and games – anything that could fill the social void in my life. I was acutely aware that we couldn't afford these finer things, so I spent every waking moment dreaming up ways to create my own income.

My first foray into self-employment was a scone-making enterprise. I was eleven years old. I would wander the streets of my hometown, Lara, with a pen and paper, taking orders for fresh scones. Once I had filled the page with orders, I would head home and bake them with Mum, wrap them in a towel, and deliver them with a tub of jam and cream. I still remember the price: six scones for $10. And the best part was Mum bought all the ingredients and paid for the electricity to bake them. With zero cost of goods sold and operating expenditure, it was the most profitable business I've ever run!

My next business was Andy's Lawn Mowing Service. I charged $10 for the front yard, $10 for the back. Again, I coerced Mum into buying the petrol and supplying the mower, so I was on a sweet wicket. I wasn't smart enough to pick the smaller yards, though; I remember some guy's eyes lighting up when I offered to clip his three-quarter-acre block with my push mower for twenty bucks!

I also enrolled in the obligatory paper round on my bike, on the very day I hit the eligible age of 12 years and 9 months old. I pedalled like a kid possessed all over our sparsely populated town, milk crates bouncing on the front and tied down with Occy straps. I beat the pavement in all weather conditions from 4.30 in the morning, six days a week for $18. Then, after twelve months (thanks to Mum managing the newsagency), I eventually got promoted to selling papers in the train station kiosk, starting before the 5.40am express to Melbourne and finishing up after the 8.20am service. The money was better, I was out of the elements and I didn't have to exercise, so it ticked all the boxes.

It was no surprise to anyone that I decided to drop out of school in Year 10, a few months short of my sixteenth birthday. I don't recall getting much resistance from the school, who were at a loss to know what to do with me, but Mum and Dad were fiercely determined to keep me in the school system. They saw it as a form of daytime incarceration, and were fearful of how I would spend the extra time I had on my hands. Eventually they relented, coming to terms with the fact that no good was coming from my reluctant attendance at a school of troublemakers. Their proposal was this: find yourself a full-time job and you can leave.

After years of railing against the system, I had been granted my wish. But with little formal education, no circle of friends to rely on and more than a few destructive tendencies, the chips were stacked against me. I felt completely misunderstood and alone in the world. But, like many others with ADHD, I had a fierce energy and passion inside me that I could feel deeply.

Once I was able to unlock that energy and harness it in a positive way, the rest, as they say, is history.

Chapter 2

Mentor or Tormentor?

Since I was eleven years old, joining the workforce and earning money was all I wanted to do.

I had over forty jobs between the ages of twelve and twenty-four, many of them overlapping, and I loved (almost) every minute of it. I worked in newspaper deliveries, fast-food chains, office administration, project management roles, door-to-door sales, and I even handed out tasting samples for a food and beverage company when I lived in Ireland. I was never too proud to do any type of work in the pursuit of income, and happily cleaned the mud out of the car wash bays at the APCO service station in my hometown of Lara as a sixteen-year-old. I was given the nickname 'Middle of the Day Man', because I could be called upon at any time of the day or night (for a pre-negotiated surcharge, of course) to remove the large deposits of mud left behind by a group of ute-loving locals.

My first full-time job after leaving school was in the putty and sand division of a timber furniture company. The wage was $4.72 per hour, the work was hard and my boss, Cookie, was an absolute tyrant. He would march aggressively around the workshop floor and force me to lean back as he launched into a withering verbal attack that came with a free shower of spittle. Everyone hated him, and we were spurred on purely by the need to put food on the table.

The $152 that I took home per week was the shining light of that job, funding my insatiable appetite for party pies, chocolate milk and Moro cigarettes. I also loved the commute into work, confidently striding onto the train in my KingGee overalls and feeling a sense of pride I had never experienced before. I used to finish the workday by smearing putty on my overalls and covering myself in sawdust, crafting an image of someone who had done an honest day's work.

Working for a terrifying figure like Cookie taught me that while I could get away with backchat at school and home, it wouldn't fly in the workplace. I regularly had to stand there and cop an absolute spray in front of my co-workers, feeling completely denigrated but too fearful to talk back. While it felt horrible at the time, it started to shape my future self and set me on a path that looked far more desirable than the one I had been headed on six months earlier.

It also became a common theme of my professional life: in every place I worked during those twelve years, I learned more about how *not* to run a business.

I'll never forget the feeling of being completely disengaged, unappreciated and realising that your boss couldn't care less about you as a person. After a turbulent but formative six months as Cookie's whipping boy, I moved jobs a handful of times in less than two years. I gained valuable knowledge and insights from each position then quickly moved on once I felt I had nothing more to learn from my role (or my boss). Looking back, that desire to take what I needed and then move on to something else, rather than treading water in a job that wasn't aiding my development, was pivotal. Each of those experiences added something that I would leverage throughout my own business journey later on.

When I was seventeen, a guy in our street took a shine to me and decided to take me under his wing. Rick was a highly successful car salesman and a part-time singer. He reminded me of an old-school crooner, being blessed with an incredible singing voice and a healthy dose of charm. Rick also had an incredible ability to connect with people; he was a larger-than-life character who made a big impact on any room he entered. He oozed charisma and could tell a story or joke like no one I had ever met. Sometimes he would stand on the bonnet of a car, flapping his arms or imitating someone flawlessly to accentuate the tale, leaving his audience in stitches. He was also a deeply flawed character and suffered from his fair share of lifestyle vices, but I watched him drive home from work every day in different luxury cars, living a freewheeling life of privilege, and I wanted to be him.

Rick's nickname for me was 'Dooey' (short for Andrew), and he saw something in me – a 'gift of the gab' that he could craft into a junior version of himself. He gave me a job at a luxury car dealership in Melbourne, employing me to clean the cars and promising to guide

15

my progression through the company. I'll never forget the feeling on my first day, the spine chills I felt as I was greeted by row after row of gleaming Bentleys, Maseratis, Rolls-Royces and Lamborghinis. I was allowed to drive them around the warehouse, and I spent many hours with a soapy sponge in my hand, caressing these breathtaking vehicles and polishing them into works of art.

Eventually, Rick let me take the cars down to the local petrol station. I was eighteen years old, tearing down the road in a convertible Porsche or Ferrari with the top down, and I felt like the king of the world. The owners of the dealership were probably billionaires, a self-made Jewish family who had survived the Holocaust and gone on to achieve incredible business and philanthropic success in Australia. Their list of clientele was a 'who's who' of the Melbourne sporting, business and political scene, and for me as a young and impressionable bloke, it was intoxicating to be in their orbit.

Rick was sometimes my mentor and sometimes my tormentor. Every night he would drive me back down the highway after work, with Foster's Light Ice beers sitting on the back seat, and he would fill my head with his ideas on how I should live my life, his opinions becoming stronger and more assertive as the empty beer bottles started clinking on the floor. When we turned into our street, he'd finish his 45-minute sermon by slapping me on the back and saying, 'Anyway, Dooey, you listen to what I say and you'll be a winner.'

Having not had much of a relationship with my dad at this point, I soaked up Rick's words of wisdom like a faithful subject.

The job at the dealership also allowed me to make the move out of home and up to Melbourne, escaping from the Geelong fishbowl which had me swimming with the same troubled kids for many years. Geelong is a vibrant and booming city now, but back then it was the kind of place where you had to create your own entertainment, which was not ideal for a teenager with my tendencies.

Moving to the city opened my eyes to what the world had to offer. I gave up smoking and improved my diet, and I threw myself back into footy and cricket, which I had cast aside, along with many other good habits, in my early teens. I played footy in the reserves for Strathmore in the Essendon District Football League, where I was known for being the fittest bloke at the club, but very close to useless. I would win the beep tests against former AFL players and represent the club at the half-time grand final sprint. Then I would spend three-quarters of the game on the bench, come on for ten minutes, kick the ball out of bounds a few times and get dragged again. The coaches could only shake their heads at how someone could have all the physical attributes – six feet, a big frame with strong hands and the petrol tank to run all day – and still be an absolute liability on the field. As my wife said to me once: 'You'd be great at footy if they took the ball away.'

I loved my time at Strathmore, even if my lack of ability made it hard for me to fit in with a bunch of star footballers. After largely keeping to myself for the first half of the season, I summoned up the courage to attend the mid-season ball. I was chuffed when a couple of the senior players came over and started making conversation, asking me all sorts of questions about my footy career and generally showing plenty of interest in me. As they were smiling and nodding,

I saw their eyes dart downwards and, following their gaze, I saw the seniors captain, Doggy, lying on his back under the table with a lighter, grinning at me while setting my shoelaces on fire! Despite escaping the troubles from my school years, I was still an easy target.

Once I made the move out of home, everything started to look more promising. My relationship with Dad improved significantly, and after years of drifting between groups of outcasts, I found myself building solid and meaningful friendships. I moved into a slightly insane but incredibly enjoyable share house with some uni students, where I developed some deep friendships that would last the next twenty years and beyond. We developed a reputation for throwing epic house parties, which kept increasing in size as the word spread around Melbourne. Eventually we had to call them off after they spilled out of the house and took over the surrounding streets.

After twelve months at 'Rick's finishing school', and with a new perspective on life, I was getting restless again. The lifestyle was great, but the hours were long and the pay was rubbish. I asked the owner for a pay rise and his response was, 'I didn't become rich by giving money away', so I took that as a no.

The following week, Jason, the guy who supplied our automotive batteries, dropped in. He mentioned that he and his wife, Nicky, had dreams of building an empire but needed a good sales rep to grow the business with them. We spoke for an hour and there was a powerful connection; I found his passion and drive intoxicating. He also offered me the pay rise that had recently been dismissed out of hand.

I slept on it, and the next day I handed in my notice. Rick was gutted. He was a strong and intimidating character, and having to look him in the eye and stay true to my decision was one of the most challenging things I had ever done. I owed him so much for the faith he had in me when it wasn't apparent to anyone else. I will forever be grateful for his guidance, but it felt like the right time to move on.

It was time for a new career, and a new mentor.

Chapter 3

Here Comes the Sun

The year 2001 defined the rest of my life in a number of positive ways.

Professionally, everything was starting to come together. After spending the first part of my life heading down the wrong track, the past few years had left me feeling that my career path was now laid out in front of me. Rick had invested heavily in my development, which had given me the first real sense that I was capable of much more than what I had shown thus far.

Up until then, the main reason I had been obsessed with business was to make money and buy things. I loved fast cars with big engines and I churned through single-use packaging without a care in the world. I didn't make any effort to recycle and I was quite dismissive of anyone who cared about the environment. I had no awareness of sustainability or the impact I was having on the planet, and the thought of a higher purpose had not become apparent in the slightest.

I started working at Battery Stop for Jason and Nicky, and from day one it felt like I was part of the family. We had a deeply emotional connection and it gave me a sense of purpose that I had never experienced before. During the day, we worked on growing the business together. And after hours, I had dinner with their family and we would go water skiing or go-karting together. It was less a job and more a lifestyle. Many of my previous bosses had left me feeling like they couldn't care less about me as a person, and as a result, I couldn't care less about them or the company. Jason and Nicky taught me a very valuable lesson: if you care about your people, they will care for you, and they will go above and beyond in their jobs.

We created the slogan 'Batteries for Everything', and Jason and Nicky made a massive investment to open a showroom and factory on the Hume Highway in Campbellfield, in the northern suburbs of Melbourne. We branched out into battery recycling, selling reconditioned batteries and offering batteries for every application. Trucks, buses, caravans, video cameras, hearing aids, you name it. We signed a contract with almost every car dealer in the Melbourne metro area, cornered the caravan and motorhome market, and had a virtual monopoly on scrap battery collection in Victoria. We started recruiting heavily, and at the age of twenty-one I found myself managing over twenty-five employees, including salespeople, truck drivers and factory staff. For all intents and purposes, it felt like we were running the business together.

There was an element of 'old-school' about the business – scant regard for systems and processes, and a team that was almost entirely driven by the need to have fun every day. We built an incredible culture, despite some structural shortcomings. Business was booming and we were flying by the seat of our pants. It was intoxicating to be a part of.

But there was a problem. I still couldn't care less about what I did. Batteries are hardly the kind of product that light a fire in your belly, or something you can sit around and talk about passionately until the wee small hours (although sometimes we did!).

One day, a customer came into the shop to buy a deep-cycle battery to run his electric fence. He was grumbling about having to keep bringing the battery back to the shed (500 metres away) to recharge it once a week, and asked if I had any better options for him. I did some research online (Google wasn't well known back then so I used WebCrawler) and came across the idea of using a solar panel to charge a battery. It sounds so obvious these days, but back in 2001 there was almost no market for solar cells, and it wasn't immediately apparent as a solution. I found out I could supply him with an 80W solar panel and a charge controller, fix it to the fence, and that would keep the battery charged all the time. I could also buy the panel for $800 and sell it for $1100, which was a handy upside!

I rang the customer back, he bought the solar panel and I showed him how to install it. I connected the cables up, brought the panel out into the sun and it all came to life.

A chill ran up my spine. It was like magic.

After he left, my ADHD-fuelled mind went into overdrive. I started thinking about all the applications we could find for solar panels and the opportunities we could leverage. I frantically scribbled notes and drew up lists of the different business channels for solar. The business model revolved around water pumps, caravans, camper trailers, remote shacks and properties. At this point, installing it on grid-connected homes wasn't even part of the plan. With the exorbitant price of solar panels and relative cost of grid electricity, it was still too far-fetched an idea. I was captivated by the pure simplicity of powering anything, any time, from the sun, for free. And without any noise or moving parts.

From that moment on, I had found my mission.

I figured the easiest way to get my head around the industry was to roll my sleeves up and get out into the field, so I started by finding out what kind of licence or accreditation you needed to install these systems. It turned out that most of the applications I was interested in could be installed by practically anyone. This became a blessing as well as a curse for the emerging solar sector, allowing anyone to get into the industry without any training, but causing a tsunami of poor workmanship and incredibly dangerous wiring that would need to be cleaned up in the future. Some of the first systems we saw were staggering, with live cables dangling down from the roof and sensitive electrical components pushed into the corner of leaky sheds. It was a minor miracle that no one had been seriously injured or killed.

I figured the other way to fast-track my involvement in the industry was to build my network and find others who were already on the same journey. I asked around the traps and came across a handful of guys who were installing solar and batteries for off-grid homes in the hills. I picked up the phone and called them for a chat. Their responses were varied, to put it mildly. Some were warm and welcoming, and keen to impart their wisdom on a kid who was thirsty for knowledge and wanted to follow in their footsteps. Others were guarded and instantly treated me as a threat to their livelihood. For all the change we have seen within the solar industry over the past twenty years, that difference in mindset is still apparent.

One of the friendliest guys I met was Warwick from Kinglake. He was a lovely bloke, very passionate about renewable energy and happy to see someone like me sharing that passion. He took me out on the tools for a few installations, packing us a couple of sandwiches and a thermos full of coffee as we headed into the hills, and provided me with a hands-on masterclass on how off-grid solar works. I spent my days under houses, inside roof cavities and crawling through spider-infested sheds as I soaked up his knowledge and learned the ins and outs of these systems.

Warwick seemed to relish my burgeoning enthusiasm for solar and invited me along to a meeting with other solar installers in Victoria. It was called ATRAA, which stood for the Appropriate Technology Retailers Association of Australia. Despite the group having been around for twenty years by this stage, there were still only a handful of installers at the meeting, whose relationships had been formed and developed over many years. As the new kid on the block, I was greeted with the familiar combination of warmth and suspicion, but I took the opportunity to soak up their knowledge and ask any questions that popped into my head, and I came away feeling like we were on the cusp of something quite incredible.

My overt enthusiasm and ambition started to get tongues wagging around the industry and I found that some people became more guarded and less helpful as I started winning a few jobs. It is to be expected in business of course, but I was naive in those days and just assumed everyone would want to help. There were several people who took me under their wing and spent many hours helping to build my understanding of the industry, and I am eternally grateful for that.

Jason and Nicky were happy to indulge me in this newly discovered passion, but as the bankrollers of my new enterprise, they understandably maintained a healthy dose of scepticism. After I sold a few solar panels (and made a healthy margin), I negotiated a deal to buy twenty panels and put them in the showroom (at a capital outlay of $15,000) without telling them. Jason was shocked and upset with me when the pallets turned up, but I promised him I would sell all twenty of them within a month. It took me two weeks.

By this stage, we were receiving the odd enquiry from people who were connected to the electricity grid, but wanted to install solar to reduce their environmental footprint. It didn't make financial sense at this stage, but the early adopters didn't seem to care. They were largely driven by the environment and had enough disposable income that they could afford to do something about it. I felt like we had a great opportunity to gain an early foothold in this market, not only demonstrating that we too cared about the environment, but also tapping into another solid business channel.

I put a business case forward to Jason and Nicky to install a 1kW (six-panel) grid-connected system on the roof of our showroom, high up on tilt frames facing the highway, to show our customers that we were 'walking the walk'. I think the outlay was about $17,000 at the time.

Jason took one look at the numbers and dismissed it out of hand, and nothing I said would change his mind. I tried everything – leveraging our suppliers to reduce the system cost, getting a story in the local paper for publicity, showing him how the solar market was booming in other countries – but he wouldn't budge.

I realised at that point that we weren't aligned, and that he and Nicky didn't share my newly discovered sense of purpose. We had drifted apart energetically and now I started looking for new opportunities in the solar energy field. With a burning passion to get into this emerging sector, I knew it was time for another change of scene.

Turns out I was right – it was indeed time for a change. But it was nothing like what I had expected.

Chapter 4

Throwing It In

A couple of years earlier, I had fallen in love with something else that would shape the rest of my life. Or should I say, someone.

Kelly had moved from Gippsland to Geelong to complete her degree at Deakin University. To me, she was perfection: the ultimate combination of beauty and brains. Kel was a high performer who graduated in the top few per cent from Gippsland Grammar, and was awarded a scholarship to Deakin University in my hometown of Geelong. Kel achieved incredible results in everything she turned her mind to. She was also captivating, with a diminutive stature that was complemented by her flowing strawberry-blond hair, an effortless ability to build relationships and a spark in her eyes that drew people in. She was someone who turned heads when she entered a room – particularly mine.

Our first interaction wasn't exactly the stuff of fairytales – a hazy rendezvous in the wee small hours on the dance floor of the Geelong Hotel. But I was totally and wholeheartedly smitten by her. At the time, my life was showing some fleeting signs of heading in the right direction, but I was very much a work in progress. An out-of-shape smoker who had dropped out of school at sixteen didn't have much to offer someone of Kel's pedigree.

I was batting well above my average, and I knew it.

But there was clearly a spark between us, and after biding my time as her friend (and, reluctantly, as her relationship confidant) for a few years, she started to see something resembling a life partner in me too. I'm sure my newly acquired health and fitness regime, along with my vastly improved career prospects, played a supporting role!

As we became more serious, it felt like we had many things in common. But we had a problem from early on.

Kel was a traveller at heart. She had just returned from a freewheeling gap year in London, and nothing was going to stop her from heading back overseas and living it up when her studies were complete. Kel had already been to over forty countries by that stage, and travel was woven into her DNA.

I had never had a passport. Never even considered it.

By this stage of my life, I was deeply invested in my job and building a career, and it was all starting to take shape, so the thought of taking time off for travel had never occurred to me. Bear in mind I was twenty-one at the time, and in hindsight I had decades ahead to focus on my career. But I was so caught up in that world that nothing else seemed to matter.

Kel put it bluntly: 'If we're going to get serious and make a life together, you need to get yourself a passport.'

For someone who was as career-driven as I was, throwing in a terrific job and spending their entire life savings to travel on a tiny budget seemed like the least appealing option imaginable. But I was so completely smitten by Kel that I would have followed her to Mars if she'd asked me. I could only see a future with her in it and I was prepared to take my life in any direction as long as Kel was by my side.

Ultimately, my desire to build a life with Kel trumped my desire to build a career. So I applied for a passport and we booked a couple of one-way tickets to Ireland, heading off into an exciting but unknown future.

As is usually the case, love wins.

When I told Nicky and Jason that I was quitting my job and heading overseas with Kel, their hearts sank. They had built their professional and personal plans around me running the business and maybe taking over one day, so it was a complete shock to the system for them. Nicky was a romantic at heart, and she understood. Jason hasn't spoken a word to me since that day.

The first few days on the road were a whirlwind. I clearly remember staggering out the door of the airport terminal in Phuket, exhausted and uncertain about the decision we had made, and being hit with the sensory overload of my first Asian experience. The thick, humid air that fills your lungs. The unmistakable Thailand smell that clings to your skin, an intense fusion of pad thai, durian fruit and poor drainage. The sound of hundreds of cars, bikes and tuk-tuks barrelling through intersections, expressing themselves through their horns.

We spent our first night in a restaurant on the main street, and the rain was unbelievably intense. I'd never experienced anything like it. I stared into the dark, humid sky and pondered the decision we'd made. My chest began to tighten and I felt like I was going to cry. I remember Kel staring glumly at me from across the table, feeling guilty about dragging me on this adventure, and neither of us spoke for a very long time. The unforgettable feeling of your first bout of homesickness.

We moved on to a bar down the road and bumped into a few Aussies. With their solid builds, long blond hair and surfers' tans, they looked to be straight out of a Rip Curl commercial. They started telling us about the epic trip they'd been on, living aboard a boat for the last week and scuba diving around the nearby islands. As they regaled us with their travel tales, my eyes lit up. I started to get right into their stories and found my spirits lifting almost immediately. That session went long into the night and we ended up accumulating quite the crew by the time the bar closed, everyone laughing and swapping stories about their incredible experiences from around the world.

From that point on, my homesickness was cured. I felt an overwhelming urge to get out there and see as much of the world as my time (and finances) would allow. Once the travel bug bites you, it can be that quick, and that intoxicating.

Our next twelve weeks were spent meandering around Thailand, Cambodia, Nepal and India. Not the easiest introduction to life on the road, especially back in 2004 when there wasn't a well-beaten track for backpackers. But Kel was in her element, and it put my mind at ease.

Our life consisted of near-death experiences and a lot of fun. We survived a ride in clapped-out buses through the Himalayas. Noticing that most of the locals hopped on the roof of the bus, even when the seats were empty, I asked a Nepalese guy why they all sat on the roof.

'In case the bus, it go over,' he replied.

He let out a prolonged descending whistle, extending his hand outwards and downwards over the edge of the cliff. I followed his gaze and saw a collection of burnt-out bus shells lying in the valley, hundreds of metres below us. We joined him on the roof.

We took a sunrise boat trip along the Ganges River in Varanasi, beholding the gruesome combination of women washing their clothes and toddlers in the water, while people burned bodies on the ghats and spread the ashes into the same water about 50 metres away. It was hot and dusty, and I can't even begin to describe the smell. I vividly recall a stifling 40-degree day in Delhi, when the electricity grid went down for hours, and we were overcome by the sounds and smells of thousands of diesel generators rattling and belching out smoke along every street. That same day, an incredibly thin and frail homeless guy, who was without the use of his legs, begged me for money, and when I didn't respond, he crawled after me and tugged on my backpack, sending me flying backwards into a gutter full of sewage. This sent the nearby crowd into a fit of laughter, and left me red-faced and furious, but aware of the futility of screaming at a beggar in the streets. It was a complete assault on all the senses.

We were existing on a wafer-thin budget, which was Kel's preferred method of travel. After scrimping and saving our way throughout Asia for three months, sacrificing our need for nutritious food (but always finding enough for a few beers in the evening), we dragged our exhausted souls through the arrival terminal in Dublin with less than $250 between us. It's fair to say our planning of the Irish leg (arriving in mid-December) was poor. We had wanted to get there in time for Christmas, overlooking the fact that the recruitment agencies (and the offices of potential employers) would be closed over the holiday period. Kel had a friend who was living in a bedsit just out of the city centre in Dublin 7, and she was heading away for a few weeks. Thankfully, she offered us her place to stay while we found our feet.

'Finding our feet' took a lot longer than we had hoped, with no recruitment agencies open until late January, and the pubs having very few shifts available. It was brutally cold, we didn't know anyone and we were becoming increasingly miserable. Christmas (my first away from home) was particularly hard for me. When Kel's friend came back and sent us packing, we were nearly flat broke and up the proverbial creek without a paddle. We found a 32-bed dorm room in a hostel for €16 per night each, lobbed our entire pile of possessions into the corner of the room and stared silently at the wall for what seemed like an eternity.

To make things worse, Kel had picked up a horrible infection called giardia in India (a parasite which lodges in your intestine), which forced her to make an unexpected detour for a few days at the Hospital for Tropical Diseases in London. I'll spare you the gory details, but let's just say it wasn't conducive to pounding the pavement around Dublin for hours on end with a resumé in hand.

Eventually we found minimum-wage jobs in a pub to keep the bank account ticking over. I landed in an expat bar called The Woolshed, which was full of fun-loving and mildly insane Aussies and Kiwis, whose sole purpose for working was to fund their lifestyle. The pay was terrible, but I loved every minute of it. Kel scored a job at an upmarket pub called The Duke on Grafton Street, which attracted a much higher-class clientele. Kel's spectacular strawberry-blond hair was a massive hit with the Irish and, combined with her natural ability to charm the customers, she absolutely cleaned up on the tips. This was in the glorious economic period of 2004–05, as the Celtic Tiger was roaring at the top of its lungs, and the American tourists in particular were incredibly generous. Kel used to collect her tips in her apron and would wake me up in the wee small hours when she came home. We would excitedly pour the coins out all over the bed and count them up. Some nights she made over €100, which was around double what she made in wages.

Over the next eighteen months, we popped in and out of Ireland several times. We returned and worked when we had to, sometimes after running down to the last few hundred euros between us. And when we replenished the bank balance to something moderately sustainable, we dropped everything and hit the road until we found ourselves at financial rock bottom again.

On that trip, we lugged our backpacks around fifty countries throughout Asia, the Middle East, Western and Eastern Europe. We went hiking, rock climbing and scuba diving, and embraced anything that contained an element of adventure or danger (and preferably both). We survived a number of near-death experiences (including the time when we went rock climbing with a couple of Spanish guys, and Kel dislodged a boulder above me, which hit my backpack and *very* nearly sent me tumbling 200 metres down a snow-covered cliff face to a premature end).

Some of our most dangerous moments on the road were the result of my cavalier attitude, and quite stupid in hindsight. I've had a knife pulled on me in a Vietnamese hostel, and been chased up the street by a cab driver with a hunting knife in Brazil, after he tried to rip me off on the cost of a trip. Despite having had my wallet stolen on two separate occasions, I maintain a 2–0 record, having recovered it both times from the perpetrator without losing a cent. The first time was late at night on the main tourist strip of La Rambla in Barcelona, when a bloke came up to me and asked if I was English. 'Ooh, you know David Beckham. You like football?' he said, and he started kicking my feet playfully. I swatted him away and felt the lifting of my wallet from my back pocket by his accomplice. They took off at breakneck speed.

There was only €20 in the wallet, but I'd had just the right amount of sangria. I liked my chances. I tore off after them and Kel bolted in pursuit of me. As they turned into the dark laneways off the main strip, Kel was screaming at me to stop, concerned they were leading me into a trap. But I was gaining on them and in no mood for calling off the chase. I caught the first bloke, the decoy, who leaped into the bushes and left his mate to fend for himself. The thief shot a terrified glance behind him as he turned into another laneway, and upon realising that I wasn't likely to give up, froze in place with his back against the wall. He launched my wallet into the darkness, curled up in a ball with his hands in front of his face and squealed in a high-pitched voice, 'No trouble, no trouble!' Having got what I came for, I resisted the urge to teach him a further lesson and let him scamper off into the darkness. I came back to greet Kel, marching back with my wallet held up in the air like a triumphant warrior. She wasn't impressed.

We overcame many illnesses and trips to the local hospitals, and experienced some of the highest and lowest moments of our lives. We also built some amazing friendships, creating a deep level of connection that can only be forged when you are thousands of kilometres from home. Twenty years later, many of those friendships are as strong as ever, and we have been all over the world to reconnect, introduce our children to each other and reminisce about our time spent on the road together.

Considering how materialistic I had been in my early years, travel taught me a valuable life lesson about what truly matters. We didn't have much, and we didn't need much. It almost became a source of pride to see how much fun you could have on a shoestring budget, and it fundamentally changed my values for the better. I was also shocked by the indifference that people in many countries have for the environment, driven by either a lack of policies or a general lack of awareness, and it infuriated me to see pollution choking the air, or piles of trash building up in streets and waterways.

By now, it was clear I had been bitten by the travel bug. We returned home, thoroughly exhausted, and seemingly ready to resume our career ambitions. We got married, bought a house and tried to settle into a 'normal' life. That didn't last long, and before we knew it, we had a tenant in our house and we were back on the road again, this time covering the length and width of South America over five months. We swayed in hammocks in a slow boat up the Amazon River – which sounded idyllic. Think seven days sleeping in a hammock, suffering from crippling food poisoning and rushing to the toilet, with each frequent trip disturbing the passenger in a hammock above and below me. We went scuba diving in old volcano craters on the Galapagos Islands, and suffered from brutal altitude sickness while climbing a 6000-metre peak in Bolivia without oxygen.

Travel is hard. It's particularly hard as a backpacker when you have to find the cheapest way to do everything, and you are a very long way from the security blanket of home and family. But I cannot overstate the value of those life lessons and how they can literally change you as a human being. My two favourite character traits are *resilience* and *positivity*, and like in life, developing those traits can make or break your experience on the road. Some of the worst days of my life happened during those travel years, but when you go through these setbacks day after day, you develop a very thick hide and eventually learn to accept them as part of the experience.

Some of these setbacks took us on paths we weren't expecting, exposing us to new places, people and experiences that were incredibly enriching. I remember arriving at a train station on a freezing evening in Plovdiv, an ancient city in Bulgaria. It was peak winter, no one spoke English and the street signs were written in Cyrillic. We were broke, homesick and couldn't find anyone who could help us track down a bed for the night. A lady named Maria came up to us and, noting the glum and defeated look on our faces, asked us (in hand signals and very broken English) if we needed help.

Back in the mid-2000s, there was very little tourism infrastructure in Plovdiv, and we literally couldn't find a place to lay our heads for the night. She beckoned us to her car, drove us to her home on the other side of the city and made us a cup of tea. We sat there awkwardly at her kitchen table for fifteen minutes, while she shuffled around the house. Maria emerged with a huge smile on her face and ushered us to her spare room where she had made up the bed for us. She whipped up a lovely meal of Bulgarian meatballs, then invited every member of her extended family over to meet her new Aussie backpacker friends. We all smiled awkwardly around the dinner table and exchanged pleasantries (reciting some phrases from the *Lonely Planet Bulgaria* guidebook we had with us). Once the conversation dried up, Maria turned on the TV and found re-runs of *Friends*, which had Cyrillic subtitles. We watched a few episodes and laughed at the same moments, nodding at each other as a form of conversation. We bid the visitors farewell, then crawled into a warm bed and drifted off to sleep.

The next morning, Maria found us some respectable clothing and brought us to her church, where we met her congregation, said a few prayers with her and lit some candles. It was a deeply moving experience and a complete immersion in Maria's culture and way of life. I still remember those few days as one of my richest travel memories, and it had all started with a healthy dose of uncertainty and adversity.

The learnings from those years on the road ended up defining the rest of my life and contributed significantly to the success in the rest of my professional career. To anyone who is considering a stint living or travelling abroad, a gap year or a mid-career sabbatical, my advice is to just back yourself in and do it. There are some lessons in life that can only be learned by stepping out of your comfort zone and hitting the road. It accelerates all of the positive elements you need in life: resilience, empathy, compassion and tolerance. Go and eat at a dodgy-looking restaurant with the locals and sit on plastic chairs. Strike up a conversation everywhere you go. Say yes to every opportunity or experience. Learn the language, and when you have exhausted your knowledge of the language, remember that a smile is universal. And don't focus purely on the destination, just enjoy the journey.

I loved this stage of our lives so much and it had me wondering if my priorities had changed permanently. It was quite remarkable to go from where I had been at twenty-one, materialistic and obsessed with career progression, to where I was in my mid-twenties, flat broke and struggling to top up the mortgage repayments, but blissfully happy to be living a life full of adventure.

Eventually we decided it was time to 'grow up' and return home, build some solid foundations and prepare for what we hoped would be the next stage of our lives – as parents.

Once we were back, my career ambitions clicked into gear. And like everything I had done to this point, it was headfirst and at full speed. I threw myself back into the solar industry, which had begun to mature and evolve from a cottage industry. A few strong players had emerged and there was a sense that something was brewing.

None of us could have imagined what lay ahead.

Chapter 5

Finding My Wolf Pack

My return to a 'normal' life in 2007 coincided with the first incredible wave of rooftop solar uptake in Australia.

Back in 2001, when I started in the industry, even the most unwavering optimist could not have imagined what would transpire over the next two decades. It seems inevitable now, with Australia having the highest penetration of rooftop solar in the world, but here are a few statistics that will help you realise how niche the solar industry was in 2001:

- There was a grand total of 118 rooftop solar systems installed across the entire country. (Now we have over 3.5 million!)
- The average system size was a measly 1kW (6 x 170W panels). (Now it's around 8kW.)
- That 1kW system would cost around $17,000 installed, and

pay for itself in around fifty years. (Now an 8kW system costs around $8000, and the ROI is closer to four years.)

The federal government had brought in a renewable energy target in late 2001, with a $4000 rebate to install a 1kW system, but that did nothing to move the needle. Solar panels were still far too expensive, and grid electricity (dominated by brown and black coal) was abundant and relatively cheap.

In 2007, just before he was voted out of office and just as I reignited my career in solar, Prime Minister John Howard turned the industry on its head. He announced the Solar Homes and Communities Plan (SHCP) and doubled the rebate to $8000 for a 1kW system. Why they didn't alter the rebate to $8000 for a 2kW system, generating double the output for the same taxpayer investment, was beyond me, but it was the first of many puzzling policy decisions that would take place in the energy space in the years ahead.

Anyway, this new rebate scheme opened the floodgates and our cottage industry became a serious force almost overnight. The free market forces were in full effect, driving the out-of-pocket expense down from $4000 to $1000, and eventually putting a system on the roof for no cost. I still remember picking up the newspaper one day and seeing one of our competitors on the front page, offering a free 1kW system AND a $1000 Coles–Myer gift card. You can imagine what this rapid rise did for standards and quality, with everyone wanting to get on the gravy train, and companies appearing and disappearing at a frantic rate.

I desperately wanted to be a part of this revolution, and to work for someone reputable who aligned with my values. A vacancy opened up for a sales manager position at The Environment Shop, which was the pre-eminent company in the sector at the time. They started as an environmentally friendly retailer – selling everything from solar panels to batteries, non-toxic floorboard oils to compostable nappies – and had a lot of credibility and authenticity. The company was founded by Mick Harris, one of the original trailblazers of renewable energy. Mick founded the Alternative Technology Association (ATA) and wrote the first *Renew* magazine. He did some amazing work in East Timor, donating solar and battery systems to provide lighting in remote villages. Mick was an absolute pioneer and someone I had (and still have) an immense amount of respect for.

Evidently, I wasn't the only person who was keen to jump on the 'solar coaster'. They had over 100 applicants for the role and it took a bit of resumé embellishment to even get on the shortlist for an interview with Mick and his office manager, Cass. I had done a mountain of research on the company, and on Mick personally, and brought every bit of charm and enthusiasm I could muster. I was the last applicant to be interviewed and they asked me to step out of the room for ten minutes when we were done.

I came back in. Cass flashed me a broad grin: 'Well, we like you.'

I had the job on the spot. I skipped home, punching the air.

It was a baptism of fire when I came in for my first week. There were hundreds of projects on the go, and everyone was exhausted but extremely driven to succeed. It was my first big lesson in company culture; Mick had assembled a team who cared deeply for the work they did and everyone was completely invested in the mission of changing the world. Nobody seemed to mind the relentless hours and pressure of the job, because they saw it as a purpose.

I felt completely out of my depth and my imposter syndrome went into overdrive. Everyone had degrees and qualifications and I was surrounded by some of the sharpest minds and highest achievers I had ever met. But I had earned myself an opportunity, so I decided to fake it until I could (hopefully) make it.

I developed some lifelong friendships in that role, and several of them went on to work for me in the years ahead. We were the shining example of a 'broad church', with everyone bringing something different to the table. Richard, our project manager, was my offsider; I would manage the sales and he would manage the project delivery. Richard was one of the most intelligent and gifted people I had ever met, but he had a shocking temper (especially before his morning coffee). Often, I would be sitting on the phone, trying to pacify a customer with all the polish I could muster, and he would be in the background, providing unfiltered advice that he wanted relayed to them. I learned to place my hand over the mouthpiece when I wasn't speaking so that Richard's feedback was never received directly. I frequently had to pose as the owner of the business to pacify disgruntled clients, acting as the mediator for Richard before it escalated to Mick.

We worked hard, and we partied hard. Every Friday afternoon at 4.30pm, we would fire up 'Under Pressure' by Queen and David

Bowie on the office speakers and we would stand on our desks, arms aloft, belting out the lyrics at the top of our lungs.

Then we would migrate across the road to the Bender Bar and toast another successful week with jugs of Coopers Pale Ale, and plenty of hugs, laughs and dance floor huddles. These sessions would go well into the night, and I remember them fondly as some of the best days of my working life.

Within a few months in the role, things were about to go to another level. The newly elected Rudd Labor government realised it had inherited a problem, with no cap being put on the solar rebate scheme. We were quickly heading towards 100,000 systems approved under the rebate (at a cost of $800 million), with 90,000 of those applications coming in the last eighteen months. They had to do something.

I shuffled into work late on a Monday morning, slightly groggy from a big night and with my phone on silent in my backpack. I turned into High Street and stopped to rub my eyes. There were *hundreds* of people queuing up outside The Environment Shop, the line snaking up the street. One of the admin team was rushing back and forth along the crowd, handing out coffees from the bakery across the road.

'What's going on?' I asked her.

'The government has just killed off the solar rebate. It finishes at 5pm today! Anyone who has an application in by then can still claim it.'

The rest of the day was a whirlwind. Mick called everyone he knew to come and help for the day. We set up a makeshift office with six desks and we punched out hundreds of generic quotes for a 1kW system, asked the customer to sign it, and put it in a pile for processing. There was paperwork flying everywhere, but we got it all in by 5pm. That's several million dollars' worth of jobs in a day! We then called every electrician on the accredited solar installer list and spent the next three months installing the systems.

At the same time, local councils started getting on to the idea of solar 'bulk buys' for their ratepayers. We were the go-to company for most of this work, and I learned some valuable lessons on how to scale a business quickly while maintaining a certain level of standards. We didn't always get it right, but we were blessed with a terrific team and we all had each other's backs.

On top of this, the government also announced a longwinded but popular program called the Remote Renewable Power Generation Program (RRPGP). It was basically an incentive for off-grid homes to use less petrol and diesel generators, offering a whopping 50 per cent rebate for off-grid solar and battery systems. The program was incredibly effective, but as it was essentially uncapped, it didn't take long for the market to abuse the system. An off-grid package that should have cost about $30,000 was being quoted at $50,000, with half of the price coming back as a rebate. Systems became way bigger than they needed to be, and margins went through the roof. It wasn't direct market collusion, but it just became the 'going rate'.

I can clearly remember a day when the enormity of this revolution started to dawn on me. I walked into the warehouse one morning as a container truck was dropping off the latest delivery of stock. I looked around in amazement at the hundreds and hundreds of solar panels and inverters piled up around me, overflowing into the laneway behind our shop. It was only six years earlier that I couldn't convince Jason and Nicky to install six panels on the roof of our showroom, because it 'didn't make sense'.

Incredibly, just as the solar industry was starting to really take off, BP Solar announced the closure of their manufacturing plant in Homebush Bay, Sydney. Everyone was gobsmacked. BP Solar had a stranglehold at the time, with over 80 per cent market share. For context, no manufacturer has achieved anything beyond 20 per cent since then. At this point in time, importing solar panels was almost unheard of, and we didn't need to. Australia had the technology, innovation and production capacity to meet its own needs, with the University of New South Wales long regarded as 'ground zero' for the global solar industry. UNSW had been making and breaking world records for solar cell efficiency for several decades. All the sharpest minds in solar energy had cut their teeth at UNSW under the guidance of Martin Green, who is often referred to as the 'father of photovoltaics (PV)'. But many of these pioneers of the industry were enticed to set up manufacturing facilities in China, which meant that Australia couldn't (or wouldn't) compete with the cheap products that were starting to arrive on our shores. It's a great shame we missed this opportunity, and, as I will explore throughout this book, we are still making the same mistakes fifteen years later.

Anyway, the rooftop solar industry was booming. We were at the epicentre of it, and I never once thought of leaving that job; it was everything I could have hoped for. By this stage, Kel and I were in our late twenties and starting to think about raising a family. Kel was a country girl, born and bred on a 600-acre farm at Woodside Beach, a town of less than 100 people on the Ninety Mile Beach in Gippsland. She had a simple but fulfilling childhood, spending her early days riding bikes around the farm and building cubbies in the sand dunes. Saturdays were spent hanging around the sporting club with her friends, using their imaginations to entertain themselves, while her mum and dad played footy and tennis (and carried on well into the night).

We had a long chat about it one evening. Kel spoke about the stability of being born and raised in the same town for twenty years. She spoke fondly of the connections you build within a small community, adding layers to those relationships through volunteering roles, the bonds that develop through sporting success and failure, and the triumph and tragedy that life throws your way. She wanted that upbringing for our children, and despite never having lived in the country, I was fully on board with this idea. Kel had shaken up my life direction before and it turned out to be the best decision I had made, so she had a few credits in the bank.

I came to Mick in late 2009 and told him that I loved my job, but I wanted to move to Gippsland. I asked if he would let me open a franchise of the business (now rebranded as EnviroGroup) down there. I brought up the aerial map.

The first obvious thing he noticed was that it was surrounded by coal-fired power stations and open-cut mines. For someone who had lived his entire life in the inner green belt of Melbourne, where everyone shared a love for sustainability, opening a renewable energy business there must have seemed like pure insanity.

He rejected my proposal outright.

I thought about it for a night, then came in the next day and handed in my resignation.

We had made the decision to prioritise our lifestyle. I just hoped Mick was wrong about the business part.

Chapter 6

Greener Pastures

Once Kel and I made the decision to relocate to Gippsland, as with every life decision we made, we threw ourselves into it headfirst. Every weekend was spent traversing the region, to determine the best place to drop our anchor and build a new life.

Gippsland is a huge region of 40,000 square kilometres, equivalent to the size of Switzerland. It has an economic and population spine that runs through the Latrobe Valley and out to East Gippsland. To the south of this spine, there is over 1000 kilometres of coastline and world-renowned national parks, and to the north, several mountain ranges and a couple of snowfields. Picking a town (out of more than 200 options) to call home was a huge deal for us, as we only ever wanted to make the move once.

The first thing we decided was that while we wanted to be close to the main towns of the Latrobe Valley for the career and infrastructure advantages it provided, we had no desire to live in the valley. At the time, there were four coal-fired power stations operating and the air quality was some of the poorest in the state. What struck us was that many people didn't seem to care. Unemployment was already high (sitting at around 20 per cent in Morwell), and there was a passive acceptance that this was the price to pay for keeping the local economy ticking along.

After shortlisting a handful of towns, we fell in love with the South Gippsland township of Mirboo North at first sight. It was a picturesque village of 2000 people in the hills above the valley, straddling the top of the Grand Ridge in the Strzelecki Ranges. The main street runs along the ridge and falls away into rolling hills in all directions, and the footy ground is infamous for its 6-metre slope from one wing to the other. It has high rainfall and four distinct seasons (often in the same morning!), so the soil is incredibly rich, with farmers attracted to the fertile growing conditions that the climate provides. The region produces over 100,000 tonnes of potatoes every year, and nearby Thorpdale even has an epic Potato Festival to celebrate the history of the humble spud.

Everything was within touching distance; it was twenty minutes from the valley, forty-five minutes on any point of the compass to the major towns, and forty-five minutes from some incredible beaches. It had everything we could have asked for: a primary and secondary school with a solid reputation, a thriving sporting club and golf club which were the physical and energetic heartbeat of the town, a supermarket, pharmacy, hardware store, medical centre and a spectacular outdoor pool nestled into the fringe of the bushland. It also had a pub *and* a highly awarded brewery, which basically sealed the deal.

Our first trip to Mirboo North was for lunch at the brewery, and a local bloke came up to the bar: 'Where ya from, buddy?'

'Well, mate, we've actually just decided to move here and raise a family, so we'll be locals soon.'

'Mate, you'll *never* be a local.'

Unfazed, I pointed at Kel's baby bump. 'What about this young fella? He'll be born here.'

He lightened up immediately. 'Oh yep, he's got no worries. He'll be a local!'

After wandering the streets for a few hours, striking up some conversations and marvelling at the incredible landscape surrounding the township, we were hooked. We headed straight to the real estate window, checked out the first place that grabbed our attention (the closest house to the brewery that was for sale) and put an offer in the very next day.

Our city friends looked at us with a mixture of envy and disbelief at this sudden tree change. We hadn't done much research, had thrown in our jobs while Kel was in her second trimester and had no jobs to go to. We also didn't know a single person in town. I'd never lived in the country before, but we always figured we could just come back if it didn't work out.

I remember the day we moved into town, which happened to be Valentine's Day. I carried Kel over the threshold, we dropped our bags and boxes in the house, and I was straight off to footy training over the road to meet the boys. The sporting club is the heart and soul of every regional town, so I figured this was the best way to start embedding myself into the community. It also helps if you are handy at sport, so for someone with a clear lack of ability, it was a nerve-racking experience. I threw myself into the first session with the usual gusto, running around like a lunatic and kicking the ball over my teammates' heads repeatedly.

Our coach, Joffa, was the exact opposite of me. Hailing from a famous local family (and marrying into another one), he was blessed with more talent in his little finger than I had in my whole body. Joffa would charge out of packs with the ball tucked under his wing, blond hair flowing in the breeze as he swung onto his left foot and seemingly hit targets for fun. He was a softly spoken guy but had a presence about him, and when he did speak, everyone listened.

Joffa pulled everyone into a huddle when the session started.

'Fellas, this is Andy Mac. He's just picked up his whole life and moved here. His wife is heavily pregnant, he doesn't know anyone in town and he's looking for work. It's a huge step for them so let's make sure we get around him.' Everyone came up to introduce themselves throughout the session, and life in Mirboo North just felt right from that moment on.

Little did Joffa know at the time that we had been in a bidding war with him for the house we just bought, managing to pip him by a couple of thousand dollars. He might not have been so warm and friendly if he'd known that!

Moving to a tiny town in the hills brought so many benefits, but it wasn't all smooth sailing. The local supermarket was a huge step down from the plethora of options we had in the city, frequently running out of core items (we quickly realised that you have to base your dinner plans on what ingredients are available that day). Being pregnant wasn't easy, with a trip to the doctor for a check-up taking up most of the day.

Even my relationship with the beloved footy club got off to a shaky start.

I played the first handful of games in the seniors, got named in the best players for the first final in the reserves, and didn't miss a single game all year. Then our reserves team made it into the grand final and I was dropped for a much-loved club legend (and second-generation Mirboo Northian), who had qualified for selection just in time for the finals. I was absolutely gutted. He got injured early while I ran the water all day, watching on while we got belted on the big stage, and convincing myself that I would've made a ten-goal difference (quite unlikely).

At that moment, I reflected on the fact that indeed I might never be a 'local'.

That night, over a consolation beer, one of the senior players pulled me aside and placed a hand on my shoulder.

'Andy, I know you're hurting, but what happens from here will define you. If you dust yourself off and come back stronger next year, you'll always have the respect of the club and everyone involved in it.'

I didn't really have a choice anyway. The sporting club is the hub of the town in so many ways and there was no way I was going to throw my toys out of the cot and drive up the road to play against my hometown. I turned up on day one of training in November, worked harder than ever and had my most productive and enjoyable season. From that day on, I've never looked back, going on to play hundreds of games of footy, cricket and tennis for the town. I've loved every moment (except for losing five out of five grand finals).

What I lacked in talent I made up for in my white-line fever, and it's fair to say that my intensity cost me a lot of solar sales over the years. When I stepped out onto the sporting field, I couldn't care less about the impact on our business and did anything to win. I did have one rare moment of sporting achievement, in the dying minutes of a tied preliminary final against Yinnar at their home ground. Playing in the backline, I came off my opponent and intercepted a switch across the ground. I took off and booted it from outside the 50-metre line on the boundary, and as soon as it left my boot, I knew immediately it was going through for a goal.

As a chronic underperformer who never wanted the ball in his hands for those clutch moments, watching the ball sail towards the goal was a euphoric feeling. I proceeded to charge along the boundary line, fist-pumping the home crowd (who were still watching the ball in mid-flight) and letting them know in no uncertain terms that we were into a grand final. I don't think I sold a system in Yinnar for five years after that day!

My white-line fever has also impacted my friendships. One day, I played against my good mate Fonzie, a wild and hairy beast with a heart of gold from the neighbouring town of Thorpdale. Our lives were completely intertwined; we were president and vice-president of the cricket club, and I had been groomsman and MC at his wedding a few months earlier. We were both competitive animals and there had been a fair bit of trash spoken between us in the lead-up. I knew he'd only had a few hours of sleep before the game and I made his life a misery from the first bounce, playing a hard tagging role and getting stuck into him verbally and physically. He'd only had a couple of touches by three-quarter time, and he'd also had about enough by then. He warned me that he would drop me if I kept going. So naturally I did, and he dropped me with an almighty punch to the jaw. Things were pretty awkward for a while, but like most issues that occur on the sporting field, we eventually sorted it out over a beer and moved on.

I've had my helmet ripped off my head and thrown onto the roof of the players' box during a melee, and even been put in a headlock during a scuffle against one of our fiercest competitors – by their goal umpire! I was more than comfortable being 'public enemy number 1', but I have since mellowed and mended many of those footy bridges (although some remain unsalvageable by mutual agreement).

Later in life, I've also been lucky enough to coach my three boys at cricket and footy, play alongside two of them in the same cricket team, and umpire their games (which has impacted on our relationship more than once). One day, Ollie and Lachie were batting together, and their refusal to communicate resulted in a calamitous run-out. They both stood in the middle of the pitch and stared at me, and I had to decide which one of them to send packing. (Ollie has a fiery temper, so I took the safe option and gave Lachie out.) Coaching the two of them to a cricket premiership was the highlight of my sporting career. Dad wasn't the least bit interested in sport, meaning that our bonding only occurred through gaming on a computer screen, so I've made it my mission to be fully invested in our three boys' sporting endeavours. I've shivered through some brutally cold winter mornings as a footy umpire and endured some baking-hot summer afternoons at the cricket crease, but I've loved the stage of life where they just want Mum and Dad to watch them play (and dissect their performances on the drive home).

When we first moved to town, Kel was six months pregnant, and the only employment option was for her to continue her old marketing job in the city. We were flat broke, so she had to get up at 4.30am on Monday morning, commute three hours to the city and sleep that night on some cushions in a friend's living room. She would then commute back on Tuesday night, have Wednesday to recover, and embark on the same arduous journey on Thursday and Friday. It was hard to watch, but Kel is as tough as they come and she just got on with the job.

I did manage to find a job with a local solar installer, managing sales of solar hot water systems for him. Pete had been in the solar power industry for over twenty years, and was part of the 'old firm' of the industry who had carved out a territory and operated with few natural predators. There wasn't really any competition in those early days and the consumer didn't have much choice in who they could go with.

I tried hard to make it work with Pete, aware that there weren't any other options and we desperately needed a steady flow of income to keep ourselves afloat. But I only lasted a few months before I realised that we just didn't see business the same way and I handed in my notice without a solid plan for what would come next.

I scoured the region for other opportunities, determined to stay in the industry at all costs. But there were only one or two other solar businesses around the Latrobe Valley at the time – the emerging appetite for renewable energy hadn't yet found its way down the Princes Highway and into coal country. Local solar companies were keeping their heads above water, but they certainly weren't in a position to expand and bring someone else into the team.

I came home after the first week of unemployment and told Kel I was out of options. At this stage we were right on the financial breadline and about to welcome our first child into the world. I was worried, and I assumed Kel would be too.

Her response surprised me: 'Well, if there's nowhere to work, then there's no competition. Maybe we should start our own solar business.'

That was all the encouragement I needed.

Chapter 7

Taking the Plunge

That Monday morning, we registered Gippsland Solar Pty Ltd with ASIC. Remarkably, someone had let the name lapse a few months earlier, so we snapped it up very quickly.

We popped into the Bendigo Bank in Mirboo North and set up a $10,000 redraw facility from our mortgage. We paid $50 for a logo on a website and placed a $150 magnet on the side of my beaten-up Ford Courier (which leaked through the dashboard onto my feet when we had more than 10 millimetres of rain). We bought an invoice book from the newsagent (those orange A5 carbon-copy books with invoices numbered 01–49), with no idea how we were going to make enough sales to fill fifty invoices. Our marketing budget? A business card ad in the *Mirboo North Times* (which probably reached around 100 people) for $6 per week.

It certainly raised a few eyebrows when a solar business popped up in a village of less than 2000 people on the edge of coal country.

It's fair to say that if you had wanted to start a renewable energy business in 2010, the Latrobe Valley would be the last place you would pick. This is a region where coal was king, and the four coal-fired power stations dominated the economy, the landscape, and the hearts and minds of locals.

I wouldn't even say people hated us at this stage – I would describe it more as ridicule. When I started getting out there and explaining our vision for a renewable energy future, people would openly scoff at me. At this point, solar energy contributed less than 0.1 per cent of Australia's electricity needs, and you'd struggle to find anyone in the valley who thought it could become anything more than a niche market for greenies and lefties. If you had hosted a renewable energy conference in the valley in those days, the attendees could probably all travel there in the same car together!

With my unapologetic desire to disrupt the status quo, I didn't make many friends within the local tradie community. When I started selling the odd solar hot water system in town, a few of the local plumbers took umbrage at me for upsetting their business models. Swapping out electric hot water systems was easy work (without having to climb on a roof) and provided a comfortable living for them. There were murmurings that the whole solar thing was a 'scam' and 'solar doesn't even work in Gippsland'. But with each happy solar customer spreading the word around town, attitudes started to change and the tide began to turn. Eventually, some of the plumbers relented and started to get on board with the idea themselves.

The fact I wasn't a qualified electrician was what bothered some people the most. In the early days, there was a long-held belief that the owner of the solar company had to be the electrician, accredited solar designer and salesperson. I had completed my solar design course, but the thought of someone selling a system without having an electrical ticket was incredibly jarring for the 'old firm' of the industry. One electrician even ran a campaign in my local paper, proclaiming: 'Buy your solar from a tradesperson, not a salesperson'. I'm sure that the CEO of Emirates isn't a qualified pilot either, but I guess that point would be lost on some of them.

It didn't help that I was quite handy at sales and marketing. One day we attended a sustainability event alongside another solar installer, and we ran a full-page advertorial in the local paper at our own expense. He came marching over to the stand, in front of the organisers and some customers, and snarled, 'It's hard to justify coming here when you go and *hijack* our event'– and to emphasise the word 'hijack', he shoved the paper in my chest. As he was escorted away, he delivered what he probably felt was the final knockout blow, shouting, 'You're not even a f—king electrician!'

I may not have been a 'f—king electrician', but I did recognise the value of being on the tools myself. In the early days after every sale, I would wake up at 6.30am, print the paperwork, load the solar panels and other equipment into my installer's trailer and follow him to the job. The installer would give me $100 to be his assistant for the day, but it was the daily grind of being on (and in) a roof that was more valuable. I took on some awful jobs in the first twelve months through sheer desperation, and having to get inside a tiny roof cavity, face down in cobwebs, to run cabling or lift roof sheets on a cathedral ceiling was a powerful lesson. I strongly believe all salespeople need to start on the tools; it gives you a fundamental understanding of the practical challenges.

One thing I learned quickly was that I was a terrible installer and not the slightest bit handy in general. My hands are still covered in cuts from Stanley knives and roof sheets, and I couldn't pull the wrapping off a product without scratching it. I was an accident waiting to happen. I couldn't even tie down a trailer appropriately, losing the odd solar panel in transit as I bounced along the bumpy dirt tracks of Gippsland. One day I even lost the trailer itself! With no safety buffer in the bank account at the time, having to replace damaged stock due to my own incompetence was unhelpful, to say the least.

I still remember my first solar PV sale. It was for a lady called Debbie, in Tresswell Avenue, Newborough. She bought a 1.9kW system, with 10 x Suntech 190W panels and a Sunny Boy 1700 inverter. She had a brittle terracotta-tile roof, and I can still remember losing the skin on my knuckles as I prised the old tiles out of position to install the mounting feet. I had called Brian, another solar installer from further down the highway, who was a little wary of me, but agreed to install it with my help. Everything went well, but in the following few weeks when the paperwork had to be submitted, he must have decided I was a significant threat to his business and refused to send the paperwork to the electricity distributor. The customer was getting quite frustrated with me, and not only was Brian ignoring my calls, but he was also telling the customer I was to blame for the delay. It took nearly six months to get it sorted, and the customer didn't get any savings until then.

I developed a healthy rivalry with this guy, in business and in life. After one particularly unpleasant business encounter, we found ourselves in combat on the cricket pitch. I was opening the bowling and he was the opening batsman, and I had all the motivation I needed. In my first over, I steamed in and bowled three bouncers in a row at him. The third one struck him under the chin, opened him up and he fell to his knees. To his credit, he came back in after ten overs (wrapped up like a mummy). My captain had saved me a few overs for the return bout, and I tried and tried, but I couldn't get him out. We shared a beer and a laugh after the game.

We ticked along through 2010, needing to sell one solar hot water system a week and one solar power system a fortnight to keep the debts paid. It was fine in summer, but by mid-2011 I learned that no one thinks about solar in the depths of a miserable Gippsland winter. The phone stopped ringing, our $6/week marketing budget wasn't creating any leads, and our funds were quickly drying up. Kel and I made a commitment to ourselves that we wouldn't take on any further debt for the business, because we still didn't know if it would work.

At the time, the federal government had committed $2.5 billion to a program called Building the Education Revolution. New classrooms, gyms and facilities were popping up everywhere. My mate AJ was a foreman for a construction company and he rang me one day in mid-winter to see how business was going.

'Horrible, mate. Can't make a sale.'

'Well, what if I can get you a job building a new secondary school gym? I've told them you have ten years of experience as a chippy, and they'll give you $35 per hour.'

Kel and I spoke about it that night, making the gut-wrenching decision to put Gippsland Solar into hiatus to take the job. I was happy to have something secure, but I couldn't see past the next month at that stage. I had a terrible feeling that starting a renewable energy business in coal country just wasn't going to work. Maybe the doubters were right.

There were a few issues with the construction job. Firstly, I suffered from the aforementioned lack of ability and coordination. Secondly, I didn't have any tools, or even a tool belt. And thirdly, I clearly didn't have the ten years of experience as a chippy that AJ had proclaimed. On my first morning, one of the guys came over and said, 'Hey, Andy, when you come back from smoko, I'll get you to hang these architraves.'

'Yep, no dramas.'

I frantically ran around the site to find AJ. 'Hey, mate, what's an architrave?'

AJ did an amazing job of supporting me (and even turning me into a reasonable tradesperson), but I felt completely out of my depth. It did help that I had a good work ethic and a keen eye for safety, which was more than could be said for some of the other guys. There were a couple of Greek brothers who spent the morning tea break facing each other with their nail guns loaded. The crowd would cheer them on as they fired nails at each other's legs and arms, getting increasingly closer until someone called 'mercy'. At least they had goggles and helmets on. Safety first, fellas.

Throughout that winter of 2011, I still had our business phone number forwarded to my mobile. It would ring every couple of days with a lukewarm enquiry and AJ would direct me under a staircase to take the call. Every few weeks I would make a sale, and towards the start of spring, things started to look hopeful again. By the end of September, I had half a dozen jobs lined up, so Kel and I sat down for a chat. We made the decision to jump off the deep end again and fire the business back up. AJ was thrilled for me – maybe because he wasn't going to miss me on the tools! I regularly reflect on how much I owe him for the support he gave me during those challenging early times.

Once we made that decision to restart the business, we were all in. We were going to make it work or go down swinging.

As the sun came out in spring and I emerged from personal and business hibernation, there were green shoots on the horizon. There had been a few government announcements, including a generous feed-in tariff of 60c per kWh (the price you are paid for excess solar that is fed back into the grid). With a combination of the tailwinds starting to blow through the industry and my bloody-minded determination to succeed this time, we quickly found ourselves installing two to three systems per week, and some weeks we had a job on every day.

Within a few months, the garage was chock-full of pallets and stock was overflowing onto the driveway. At this stage, we still had to break down each pallet and manually unload every solar panel into my 8 x 6 metre garage, then reload them into a trailer and take them to the site. We didn't make any friends with the neighbours when the large Toll truck thundered down the narrow rear laneway, and I'm sure they all felt a sense of schadenfreude when the truck driver tried to do a narrow five-point turn one day and flattened my rear fence.

Business was good, but the marital vibe was not. Sometimes Kel would come out to her car in the garage and find herself blocked in by a pile of panels, inverters and aluminium rail. The flashpoint came in late 2011, when Lachie was eighteen months old and starting to motor around the backyard. He found his way out to the rear driveway, fell onto a roofing screw and cut his hand. I was loading a job in the back lane and hadn't noticed, but I did see a very dark and stormy look on Kel's face as she marched outside.

'Get this business out of my house.'

This didn't seem like the starting point for a negotiation, so I nodded meekly and shuffled off.

The business was in 'no man's land' at that stage. We still didn't have much money behind us, and couldn't afford a warehouse and forklift, but we needed to grow out of our third bedroom and garage. This is where the community spirit in a small town really shines through. There was a local engineering company on the edge of town, who had a huge yard and an all-terrain forklift to unload deliveries. I popped in to introduce myself to the owners, Booma and Carmelo, and explained my dilemma. They had embarked on their own business journey from the family home to a factory, benefiting from the support of other businesses, and were happy to pay it forward. We scratched out a deal where they would take all my deliveries, store them in the yard and load them onto my trailer when I needed them. And it would only cost me a slab of Carlton Draught beer a week.

I told them it would only be two to three pallets per week, and it did start off that way. But with the exponential growth of the business over the next six months, it quickly became five to ten pallets a week, and eventually ten to twenty. It almost became a second business for them, albeit a highly unprofitable one, and my slab per week was not cutting it anymore.

Booma rang me one day and cut to the chase: 'Listen, buddy. It's been great to give you a hand, but I think your business is going fine now. Time to put your big boy pants on and get yourself a factory.'

This period in late 2011 and early 2012 was terrific for the business. Work was rolling in consistently (albeit propped up by government incentives), margins were healthy, and thanks to the support of Booma and Carmelo, we had kept our overheads down without any warehousing costs beyond the weekly slab of beer.

But I never felt comfortable at any stage, especially after living hand to mouth for several years prior. I was acutely aware that if these generous government incentives were to end suddenly (as we had seen happen in the past), then our underlying business wouldn't be able to sustain significant overheads. I was drawing the bare minimum wage to keep the household bills paid and food in the cupboard, paying my fair share of income tax and putting away the profits within the business for a rainy day.

Meanwhile, many of my colleagues and competitors were living the dream. Having never been through a 'boom time' before, many of them were splashing money around like it would never end. Ten-course degustation meals with matched wines, new cars, overseas holidays – all the trappings of business success. They were also frantically expanding their businesses to capture as many opportunities as possible, afraid of missing out on their slice of the pie. Suppliers were offering increasingly high credit limits, hoping to capture a piece of the action too.

I looked around at all this happening and thought, 'What if it all ends tomorrow? How will they be able to wind things back?' It seemed like I was the only one thinking like this, and there were times when I felt like we were being too conservative.

But then suddenly, the government pulled the plug on the premium 60c feed-in tariff and slashed the amount they paid by more than half. Over 88,000 Victorians had signed up to the scheme and the cost to fund it was starting to blow out.

We had a backlog of work, but sales dried up overnight. The new transitional feed-in tariff was still a respectable 25c per kWh, but the drop was too much for many customers to swallow. Within a few months, companies had gone from scrambling to fill their warehouses, to being hugely overcapitalised and desperately needing to scale down again. They were also struggling to pay their bills.

Hundreds of companies disappeared in a short space of time

(including those of several friends of mine), leaving a trail of destruction across the industry. Consumers were left with no warranty support, and suppliers were unable to call in their significant debts.

But our strategy had paid off. By keeping our outgoings under control while things were good, we were able to weather the storm over the next six to twelve months. By the time Booma and Carmelo gave me a nudge to find my own warehouse, we had enough savings behind us to set up a self-managed super fund, using it to purchase our first product showroom and warehouse. We purchased a run-down old real estate office on the main street of Mirboo North for $250,000, and spent most of what we had left to renovate it so we looked like a serious business.

I never believed in renting our premises. Maybe it was from watching the movie *The Founder* about the story of McDonald's, where CEO Harry J Sonneborn says to Ray Kroc: 'You're not in the burger business. You're in the real estate business.' Like purchasing your own home, you are always better paying off your own property investment. And if business does slow down, you always have the option of renting the building to someone else.

I have always been a little cautious and I believe that approach has served me well over the years. But if I have enough information to make a decision and feel fairly comfortable, I am quick to execute. I don't lose sleep wondering whether I've made the right decision – it is about moving forward with absolute confidence and conviction.

There are few things more important in business than your understanding of risk. Everyone has their own risk appetite, and some people are more likely than others to back themselves and go with their 'gut feel' at any cost. I commend those who have this unwavering self-belief, but I've also seen it go pear-shaped on plenty of occasions. I also feel that being loaded with debt can lead to poor decision-making and short-term thinking.

Overall, I would consider my approach to be 'considered risk', and the purchase of our first premises is the perfect example of that. And other than our $10,000 redraw to get us going, and some novated leases on vehicles, I didn't believe in taking on debt within the business. I'm sure that cost me some opportunities for growth at times. But my primary objective has always been to put my head on the pillow at night and rest easy.

Chapter 8

Breaking the Mould

Once we opened our little showroom in town, everything started falling into place.

We employed our first staff member, a cheerful mum called Brenda. She managed any enquiries that came through the showroom, printed off the paperwork and took care of all the back-of-house functions for me. I enjoyed the freedom of being able to focus on what I loved (and was good at), although I didn't escape Brenda's relentless scrutiny of my work schedule. One day I came into the shop at midday after quoting jobs all morning and was met with a melodic yet condescending, 'Oh, look who's decided to turn up for the afternoon shift.'

Things didn't work out with Brenda, and I soon found myself enticing another friend of mine, Caroline, to come on board. Caz was the office manager for a quantity surveyor and was less than convinced about leaving a secure industry for something that, at the time, seemed incredibly speculative. Eventually Caz agreed to join us and took control of every office element of the business. She was an absolute professional and a self-confessed control freak (in the nicest possible way). We got along terrifically, and the business started to spread its wings from that point on.

One of the first people I met when we moved in to town was a lanky, bearded electrician named Damien. He could be sarcastic and a bit grumpy, but we hit it off immediately. He was the first local tradie to recognise that I could be an ally to him, and not a threat. Damien was a one-man operation at the time, helping me with ad hoc electrical work. One day, I asked him to take a week off work and spend a few thousand dollars to complete a solar accreditation course; in return, I would give him all the work I had around the local area.

'How much work do you have?'

'Well, nothing at this stage. But I'm confident.'

Damien took a leap of faith in me and spent five days in the classroom, returning with his solar ticket in hand. He was a quality tradesperson, and our relationship flourished. Over the next five years, we must have given him over 400 installations, and he went on to build a team of six installers who would spread across the region to deliver our projects. Some of those installers went on to run their own businesses. I'd say the gamble paid off for the both of us.

One thing we noticed about the market is that our main competitors were all large (mostly national) providers, who relied on their scale and buying power to overwhelm us. They had slick marketing campaigns with big budgets, and teams of subcontractors who would travel into a region, install dozens of systems and leave. We didn't have a marketing budget, and no supplier would give us credit terms, so it was incredibly tough to compete with them. One day, a guy called Stuart from Seen Agency popped into the shop and asked if I'd considered a marketing campaign on TV, radio and in the local paper. I really liked Stuart's style, so I asked him to come back to me with a proposal.

He nailed the brief. Stuart believed that our unique selling proposition was that we were a local trusted provider, which was important for two reasons. Firstly, if you had an issue with your system (which was becoming an increasingly common occurrence in the industry), we could respond far more quickly than someone from out of town. Secondly, and most importantly, because we purchased most of our materials from local wholesalers and employed a local workforce, this meant that every dollar our customers invested with us went back into the local community wherever possible. Stuart believed we could position the success of Gippsland Solar as building a new industry that would create the jobs of the future. This particularly resonated with people in the Latrobe Valley at the time, where there was a sense of impending doom around jobs leaving the region.

We devised a campaign called 'Andy from Gippsland Solar', and the premise was that we were the 'local alternative to the big solar companies'. He wanted me to be the face of the ad, and I opened every commercial with 'Hi, Andy here from Gippsland Solar'. That phrase went on to haunt me for the next five years and I couldn't turn on a radio or TV without being greeted by 'Andy from Gippsland Solar'. Unsurprisingly, I copped it wherever I went.

Driving past my children's primary school during recess? 'Hi, I'm Andy from Gippsland Solar!'

The rival spectators as I ran back into a pack on the footy field? 'Look out, Andy from Gippsland Solar!'

MCing a wedding for an inebriated crowd of mates? 'You suck, Andy from Gippsland Solar!'

But it was effective.

We had developed a few sparring partners in the industry, and regularly found ourselves coming up against a business called NRG Innovators in South Gippsland. We sold similar products and had a similar value proposition. One of the owners was a very experienced guy called Shane, a hands-on electrician with decades of experience, who was transitioning off the tools to preserve his aching joints. He knew the solar industry inside out, and as a sparky-turned-salesperson, Shane had credibility in spades. Despite crossing swords on many occasions, we maintained a healthy respect for each other. After we invested heavily into our messaging and branding, we started enjoying some success against them, and they found themselves increasingly unable to compete with us. I found out later that when Shane heard our new campaign on the radio, he said to his business partner, 'That's the ad that will sink us.'

Inevitably NRG were forced to close their doors and Shane plucked up the courage to give me a call. We caught up at The French Pear Cafe in Drouin for a chat, and he said he was tired of running his own business and wanted to put more time and energy into his family. Then he asked if he could come and work for me.

It was a huge step out of our comfort zone. There was no way we could afford Shane at the time, but I also felt that with his skills and experience, it would free me up and allow the business to flourish. Shane also ticked the most important box: he was a first-class human being, the kind of person who bled the same values that were important to me. After ruminating for a few weeks, we decided to double-down and brought Shane on board as our technical salesperson. He also became the Registered Electrical Contractor for the business.

Shane's contribution to our business over the next eight years is hard to put into words. He played a key role in employing electricians and building our in-house teams, which became our key point of difference over other solar sales companies, which tended to sub-contract their work out. This unique approach ensured we had a consistent level of workmanship and after-sales service, allowing us greater control over the customer experience. Shane helped to develop systems and processes, conduct toolbox talks so we could keep up with ever-changing industry standards, and establish Gippsland Solar as a highly successful and respected company in the industry.

With our workload increasing, we had also been contracting work out to Grant, an electrician from Alberton, who lived way down in the south-east corner of Gippsland near Wilson's Promontory. Grant started off doing some installs, then began generating leads for us through his customer base in the dairy industry. We came to a commercial arrangement for the work he brought in, and soon enough I was pleading with him to wind up his contracting business and come and work for me. Grant was incredibly committed to what we were building, and was treating it like his own business anyway.

One of my favourite stories about Grant underlines his loyalty to the business. He was driving a trailer along Loves Lane, a steep road through the hills of South Gippsland one foggy morning. Crawling along the ridge with thirty-six solar panels on board, one side of the vehicle drifted slightly into the gravel and ever so slowly, the trailer tipped over and hit the ground hard. The panels weren't smashed but would definitely have suffered from 'micro cracks'. They certainly weren't fit for sale. This was about half of our entire inventory at that stage and would've nearly bankrupted us. So Grant decided to buy them off me and install them on his own house as a way of taking ownership for his mistake. If the current owner of the house is reading this, I believe they're still working fine! Grant stayed with us all the way through the journey, going on to become our GM of Operations and overseeing one of the largest teams of field staff in the sector. Grant's growth over the past ten years has been amazing to behold, and his wife, Bec, and son, Kyle, also went on to work for us and contribute heavily towards our journey.

With Shane, Grant and Caz on board, the business grew rapidly. Soon we had an install on most days and it felt like we had some momentum. All the 'big bets' I had made in those early days were paying off, and we started feeling confident about the future.

But in keeping with the theme, another unexpected setback was just around the corner.

Having already cut the feed-in tariff in half a couple of years ago, the government made another sudden announcement to drop it by another 25 per cent, to a measly 5c per kWh. Up until this point, solar had been a 'no-brainer' for those with foresight and some capital behind them. Systems were expensive (around $18,000 for 5kW), but customers were getting no electricity bills and up to $3000 in credit per year. It was money for jam. The first reduction in feed-in tariff hadn't watered down the business case too badly, but this one really hurt. It took the return on investment out to eight to nine years, putting the brakes on our industry almost overnight.

All of a sudden, the investments that we had made into people and property were looking shaky. We were running out of money and the work was drying up again. We had to do something, and fast.

Plenty of people in our industry started panicking, thinking the sky would fall in, but this is where investing in great people pays off. I called a team meeting and we sat around a whiteboard for a brainstorming session. We quickly identified the problem: it didn't make sense to feed excess solar into the grid any longer, which meant that our ideal customer had changed. We just needed to find people who used their electricity during the day. And with systems coming down in price around the same time, it would still make sense for them to install solar.

We originally focused on stay-at-home parents, but that didn't really land in a meaningful way. Then one day I was at the real estate agency in town and I saw an ad from a national solar company sitting in the tray of their fax machine, advertising solar for business. The deal was that if you installed a 10kW system on your business, they would throw in a 5kW system on your home for free.

It was a light-bulb moment. Of course! Businesses use most of their electricity between business hours, which are sunlight hours! No one else owned that market yet, and I couldn't believe we hadn't thought of it earlier.

We got to work on a marketing campaign, and although it took a while for businesses to get their heads around the investment, we started winning a few jobs. In December 2013, we won a game-changing contract to install a 100kW system on my beloved Grand Ridge Brewery in town. In dollar terms, this was six times bigger than anything we had delivered before, and it was one of the first 100kW systems in the state. The business owner, Eric, was a very savvy businessman, to put it mildly, so it took plenty of back and forth to secure the job. But it was only 500 metres up the road from us, in the first place we visited when we fell in love with Mirboo North.

It took over two months to install that system. For context, a fully compliant system of that size would now take us five days. We were making up systems and processes on the fly, and every day posed a new challenge. It didn't help that the building was 10 metres high and the internal walls of the brewery were sprayed with liquid foam for insulation. Our poor electrician, Nashy, had to spend the best part of a week chipping the foam off so we could install the cable tray, and I can still remember him standing on a ladder with a mask and goggles on, covered from head to toe in foam.

As a landmark contract on several levels, the Grand Ridge project made some serious news around the industry. Businesses were just starting to embrace social media and our sponsored post spread like wildfire. Drones weren't commonplace back then so we had to charter a small plane to fly overhead and take some high-resolution images. It wasn't cheap!

With this proof of concept behind us, we hit the ground running. Our second 100kW system was for a powerhouse business in the Latrobe Valley called Fisher's Pallets. The owner, Lew Fisher, was a highly respected business leader in the valley, with a powerful network. Lew clearly recognised some of the same entrepreneurial attributes in me that he had himself and took me under his wing. He called me in to discuss our submission and delivered thirty minutes of constructive feedback, going through it page by page and pointing out the holes in our proposal. He must have seen my face slowly falling as I realised we weren't going to be successful, so he smiled reassuringly and said: 'Andy, I'll be going ahead with you. I just want you to understand what business owners like me are looking for.' What a champion.

When we installed the system, it became clear to Lew that our safety and compliance processes were unfit for a high-profile commercial site. Lew made some notes from his office, observing what he saw, and called me in for another chat at the end of the job. He gave me a withering spray about our approach to worker safety. When he finished, he explained that he had ended up in some hot water after an incident at his factory and wanted to do everything within his power to ensure I learned those lessons before it was too late. Lew was a towering figure and a wonderful man who continued to provide much guidance to me on our business journey. I owe him so much, and his passing in 2023 was a very sad day.

Speaking of worker safety, the job at Fisher's Pallets also resulted in one of the funnier moments of our business journey, although it was terrifying at the time. Unbeknownst to me, one of my mates, Toby, was working across the road at a transport company, with a view of our project from his office window. I received a call at 9am on the second day of the job and was greeted by a very deep and stern-sounding voice.

'Morning. Is this Andy from Gippsland Solar?'

'Yep, that's me.'

'Dave Robertson from WorkSafe here.'

'Uh, hi, Dave. How can I help you?'

'You've got some blokes working at Swan Road in Morwell?'

'Yeah, we do. Is something wrong?'

'Well, I'm watching them now and I'm not liking what I see. Matter of fact, we've got some serious problems here, Andy. You might want to come down for a little chat, because I'd suggest you're in a bit of strife.'

I gulped. 'Um, sure, Dave. I'll be there straightaway.'

Then his voice lifted.

'Hang on a minute. Is this "Andy from Gippsland Solar", the guy I see on TV all the time?' The sarcasm was dripping from his voice.

'Yep, that's me.'

'You think you're a bit of a rock star, don't you, Andy? Well, how about you come down with a signed photo of yourself and we'll forget this whole thing ever happened.'

I realised then that I'd been had.

'Hang on, who's this clown I'm talking to?'

I'd been on loudspeaker and the sound of twenty blokes laughing hysterically echoed down the phone line. Toby got me an absolute ripper that day and had me shaking in my boots. It was also a wake-up call to focus on our approach to safety.

Around this time, we had become known as a serious business with potential for growth and started to get noticed around the Latrobe Valley. There was still little appetite to embrace the energy transition in the local region, but people were at least beginning to pay attention to us. The local newspaper (which was well known for its editorial bias against renewable energy) ran a feature article on us, and we were nominated for Best New Business at the Gippsland Business Awards.

But for all the positive recognition we were enjoying, we also experienced the negatives that came as part of the package. A handful of high-profile people in the valley hated what we stood for, and as we started to make an impact, their approach evolved from ridicule into hostility. They started rolling out lines from the standard luddite playbook:

'There are no jobs in solar. Once the panels are on the roof, there won't be work for anyone.'

'It's a complete waste of money. Coal power will always be cheaper, and people won't pay more for the warm and fuzzy feeling.'

'Solar will never contribute anything meaningful to the energy mix.'

'Solar is completely useless when the sun goes down.'

Back in 2014, you could make an argument for most of these points. Solar *was* more expensive per kWh than coal-fired electricity. And with thousands of people employed in the coal-fired power stations, there was a sense that the industry had strong foundations, with several decades of prosperity ahead.

My attitude wasn't helpful either. After many years surrounded by like-minded people, I was uncompromising about what the future looked like. My attitude was essentially:

'The region is going through transition and there's nothing you can do about it. You may as well embrace it before it's too late.'

If I genuinely wanted to make an impact, it was time for a shift in my mindset.

Chapter 9

Pride or Ego?

This was around the time I started to learn what was perhaps my most important life and business lesson: the difference between *pride* and *ego*.

A healthy dose of pride has helped me throughout my entire life, and certainly to achieve our business goals. Although it can have a negative connotation, pride is incredibly powerful when you harness it effectively. Pride motivates us to work hard, to achieve greatness and (many times, in my case) to prove people wrong. I am not proud of who I was back in my younger days, and the sense of shame I carried for many years has driven me to become a better version of myself – a version I can be proud of. Pride has also helped me to make thousands of good decisions along the way. When I am faced with a moral dilemma or some form of temptation to have a quick win, I always stop and ask myself if I will be proud of my decision when I look back on it later.

The greatest example is the sense of pride you feel at the achievements of others. You might see potential in someone and invest heavily in them, watching them go on to achieve amazing things. Or you might have an employee who is dealing with some issues or demons in their life, and with support through the hard times they come out the other side and evolve into a wonderful success story. Even if no one knows that you played a role in someone's success, knowing within yourself that you did can bring a tremendous sense of pride.

Ego, on the other hand, is rarely a positive thing. It can take years to come to this realisation, but ego gets in the way of good decision-making. I speak with some authority on this issue as someone who took a long time to realise that my ego was holding me back.

Ego would have stopped me from employing many incredible people along the way, starting with Shane. He was far more knowledgeable and experienced than I was, and I would constantly defer to his wisdom in front of customers. The younger version of myself would have wanted to be the go-to person in the room on any given topic, and that turned me into a terrible micromanager. But over time, I have learned to lift others up around me, and to give them the confidence to flourish and grow within their roles.

Ego was also the reason my first public speaking gig was an unmitigated failure. I was presenting to over 300 people on a council solar program that we were rolling out. I'm not the most technical person out there and I knew there would be certain questions that would trip me up. Sure enough, I concluded my presentation and opened the Q&A session, and the first hand shot up in the audience. This guy was a retired engineer and he asked me a lead-in question which was well out of my comfort zone. But I wanted to be in control of the conversation so I tried to bluff my way through his question. He nailed me down straightaway, peppering me with questions that exposed my lack of knowledge on this particular topic. Over the next few minutes, my ego dug me into a deep hole and my face went flush with embarrassment. Faced with a question like that now, I would immediately check in my ego and respond with something like this: 'That's an excellent question, and I must admit I'm not completely across the answer. Let's catch up after the session. I'll chat with my team and we can discuss it in more detail.'

Playing on the ego of others is also a tremendous recipe for business success. In 2015, we bid for a huge commercial project through a competitive closed tender process. It was in a sector that we had never delivered a project before and we desperately wanted to win this job to secure our pipeline of work. Our competitor was one of the largest solar companies in Australia, who had far more experience and a healthier balance sheet than we did, and justifiably expected to wipe the floor with us and pick up the contract.

With only a few days until we expected to hear back from the client, we attended the All-Energy Conference, which is the largest solar gathering in the country. The sales rep from this company strode up to me while I was chatting with a bunch of colleagues, and extended his hand in a passive-aggressive manner.

'Andy, I'm really sorry, but it looks like we've got this one in the bag. I just spoke to the client.' He had a beaming smile on his face, which was clearly designed to wind me up and draw a reaction.

It was awkward for everyone gathered around and they all looked at me to see how I would respond. I took a deep breath and gave him a look of resignation.

'That's to be expected, mate. I knew we'd be up against it with you guys in the mix. Can't blame us for trying. I assume you came up with something more technical and innovative than we did.'

This stroked his ego, and an even bigger grin spread across his face. He proceeded to tell me exactly what solution they had come up with in great detail, and even alluded to the price they had gone in with. I shook his hand, congratulated him and excused myself from the conversation.

My pride went into overdrive. I went straight into the foyer and started calling my team. Armed with the inside scoop, we came up with an innovative solution to beat the other company's proposal. I called every supplier who was involved in the project, hitting them up for any savings I could find to make us more competitive. When I mentioned who we were up against, they all wanted us to win the job, so everyone came back with something to help us out.

Then I called the client. 'Graeme, I understand you guys might have chosen someone else to deliver the project and I just wanted to thank you for the opportunity to put a proposal forward. I've thoroughly enjoyed working with you regardless, and I wish you well.'

'No, we certainly haven't made a decision yet, Andy. What makes you think we have?'

'Well, the other guy has been making a few comments around the conference. He said it was in the bag.'

'I can assure you we haven't made the call yet. And, frankly, I didn't like his attitude so I'm not surprised to hear he said that.'

'Well, we'd love to work with you. If the opportunity is there to revise our proposal, we've managed to get the price down a fair bit by chatting with our suppliers and we've come up with something innovative that I think you're going to love.'

He allowed me an extra twenty-four hours to put a revised option together, and the following Monday they advised us that we had won the job.

Pride had helped me to win the contract. But if my ego had got in the way, I would have rung the other sales rep to gloat about it. It wouldn't have achieved anything. We wanted to win the job, and we won it. Calling him up to rub his nose in it would have been pointless, making me no better than him. I enjoyed a glass of wine with my team that night, reflecting on how he would feel when he found out they had lost the job to us. That was enough for me.

Ego and sales don't work well together. I have met many salespeople over the years who are driven by ego, and it rarely helps them achieve success. Time after time, we would compete with much larger and more established companies than us, and their pitch was boring and predictable.

'We're really big.'

'Have a look at how many projects we've done.'

'Our team is the best in the business.'

My approach in that situation was to simply walk in and ask: 'How can I help you?'

Sales and relationship building is not that hard. Ask questions and genuinely listen to the answers. If you ask enough of the right questions and give the customer plenty of time to talk about themselves, they will tell you everything you need to know. After five minutes, you will know exactly what type of customer they are, what their problem is and how you can find the right solution to meet their needs. There are plenty of salespeople who go in with a preconfigured sales pitch, or a slide deck so full of self-promotion that they leave no time to truly understand the client and their needs. Rather than listening, they are just waiting for a chance to speak. They might feel like they've nailed it, but they leave the client feeling very unsatisfied.

And this leads me to perhaps the most valuable lesson I have learned.

The importance of *self-awareness*.

Sometimes I become so focused on what I am trying to achieve that this 'tunnel vision' significantly affects my sense of self-awareness. I still struggle with this regularly, but even that recognition is a form of self-awareness. Over the years, I have increasingly learned to put myself in the other person's shoes and think about how they might be perceiving the conversation. I still have a long way to go, but I aim to get better at it every day. This was a huge factor in my success as a salesperson through the early stages of my career.

I feel that salespeople can be the least self-aware people in business. And the more talented they are, the less self-aware they are. They might think they have knocked a conversation out of the ballpark, but they would be shocked at how underwhelmed the customer really was.

As our business grew and the team expanded, the value of self-awareness became even more critical. I've had to manage hundreds of uncomfortable conversations and I always found that putting myself in the other person's shoes was extremely helpful. Sometimes you need to be firm and direct when the message is not cutting through, and sometimes you need to soften your approach to ensure the message lands.

After twenty-plus years in business, I've made plenty of mistakes along the way. But I always try to learn from those mistakes. As the business grew and I had to work harder to stay on top of my game, I spent a great deal of time on self-reflection. I would shut down my notifications at the end of every day and spend thirty minutes reflecting on every interaction I had. Why didn't that meeting or conversation go well? What could I have done to communicate more effectively? Was I too direct, or not direct enough? Often, I would call someone in my team to workshop what went wrong, and when I asked for some feedback, they knew I wanted straight-up honesty rather than empty praise.

By applying this process year after year, I was able to handle these conversations more effectively, and it undoubtably helped me to scale the business without losing my way as a leader.

I have worked with plenty of leaders who communicate and manage their interactions very well, and many who don't. In my opinion, leaders who jam their calendar with back-to-back meetings all day are the least effective. By rushing from one thing to another all day, they miss out on the most important part: reflecting and learning from each interaction. It's the perfect example of choosing quantity over quality.

I always leave gaps of thirty to sixty minutes in between meetings wherever possible, which gives me the breathing space to prepare for a meeting, or to recap how it went before I move on to the next issue. This means I am more present and can deliver better outcomes for everyone (including myself).

And here's my final piece of advice on ego and self-awareness – one that has been my greatest weakness for many years and is still a work in progress. If a conversation or email elicits an emotional response in you, *do not respond until you've calmed down*. Then spend that time considering what you are hoping to achieve with your response. Is it to deliver an important and necessary message, or is it just about making a point so that you feel better? If it's the latter, that's your ego getting in the way.

I've had to (respectfully) hang up the phone on senior leaders because I felt that the conversation was going off course. Don't make it about their emotional state – that will only escalate their frustration. Simply acknowledge that the conversation is making *you* a bit emotional, and you would be better equipped to come back to the discussion the next day when you've had a chance to think more clearly. Nothing good comes from a conversation in that moment, for either person.

The same applies to emails, but this one is much easier to manage. Save the response in your drafts folder and come back to it after lunch or the next day (or at least set a sixty-minute delay on your outgoing emails). If you still feel the same way, send it. But I guarantee you that you won't. It can be cathartic to put your thoughts down in writing, even if you never end up sending it to the intended target. (And if you do decide to send the same response, at least it will be more eloquent and considered than something that is fired off in the heat of the moment.)

The drafts folder of my inbox is full of emails that have never seen the light of day, and the content in this folder would make a great book in itself!

Chapter 10

The Conversation Starter

I didn't go into 2014 with much confidence that the Latrobe Valley was ready to embrace the energy transition.

But one huge and unexpected event started to turn the tide.

On 9 February 2014, after the hottest run of weather in over 100 years, a bushfire started in the grassland surrounding the Hazelwood Power Station. Fuelled by soaring temperatures, it quickly spread along the Princes Highway in Morwell, destroying dozens of properties. This included the house of my good mate Snelly, who raced home from his cricket match to watch the fire licking up the walls of his house. Fortunately, he saved the house, but it took him months to rebuild his fences and replace the damaged infrastructure on his farm.

Most concerningly, the fire spread straight into the vast Hazelwood open-cut mine.

For forty-five days in February and March, the region was blanketed in choking smoke and ash. Elderly and infirm people were evacuated from their homes, and schools and businesses were closed. At night, you could see the coal mine glowing red, and by day you couldn't see much at all. I remember playing a game of cricket against Moe in late February and barely being able to see across the other side of the field. I can't even describe the smell, but it filled your lungs and made you cough for days on end. I had a splitting headache for some time after the game. We shouldn't have been out in the open air while the mine fire was raging, but it went on for so long that people had to get on with their lives.

Over 7000 firefighters worked tirelessly to contain the fire, but the burning coal seam made it almost impossible to extinguish. The mine fire had a devastating impact on the health and wellbeing of local residents, with dozens of people treated for respiratory problems and other illnesses. It's a scar on the psyche of the Latrobe Valley that will remain with us forever.

The fire also shaped the way that the local region felt about these coal mines, reinforcing that there can be a heavy price to pay for this kind of economic 'prosperity'. The three open-cut mines (Yallourn, Hazelwood and Loy Yang) are up to 200 metres deep and occupy an area of more than 50 square kilometres (and growing). This is approximately 1.5 times the size of the City of Melbourne, and it's nearly impossible to protect such a vast area from events like a bushfire or serious storm in the future. Community groups sprung up in the aftermath of the mine fire and subsequent inquiry, and the groundswell for change started to build.

It was an incredibly emotional and anxious time, with even the staunchest advocates of the power stations acknowledging how damaging this disaster was for the community. Having upset plenty of locals with my position on the future of this industry in the past, I saw nothing to gain by getting involved in the conversation at such a sensitive time.

I regret that in hindsight.

As someone who has always believed strongly in the need for change, I should have been more courageous. The impact on air quality and health and wellbeing of the community is the most compelling reason to accelerate this energy transition. The air quality in the Latrobe Valley is some of the worst in the state in 'normal times', and the mine fire brought this critical issue to the forefront of people's minds. I shied away from engaging for fear of upsetting people, when I could have found many ways to contribute to the conversation in a constructive way.

Regardless, there was a noticeable shift in the way that the Latrobe Valley started to think about renewable energy. And we became one of the beneficiaries of this change in mindset.

Like many other organisations in the valley, we maintained a complex but fruitful relationship with Latrobe City Council over the following years. You could essentially place the people from the council in one of three groups. There was the coalition of rusted-on coal advocates who didn't like any interruption to the status quo, and believed that the transition to renewable energy was an existential threat to the region. Then there was a small cohort of people who were driven to embrace this transition and capture the opportunities, and operated in a seemingly clandestine way to accelerate the transition from the inside. These people usually had a short professional life expectancy, most of them becoming frustrated and giving up to leave for greener pastures (pardon the pun).

Then there was a new guard who sat somewhere in the centre. They were respectful of the Latrobe Valley's history in power generation, yet completely open to the idea of energy transition. They wanted to understand the challenges and opportunities in more detail. Dan Clancey and Kellie O'Callaghan were two of these people; they were passionate about the energy industry, but with a healthy dose of pragmatism and an open mind.

I remember Dan (who was standing for election to join Kellie as a councillor) giving me a call out of the blue, wanting to know if I was free that morning, and how I took my coffee. He popped in and said, 'I hear what you're saying about energy transition, and I also hear from some quarters that it will be a terrible thing for the valley. I want to understand where you see the challenges and opportunities, and what your vision for energy transition would mean for us.' I was impressed by Dan's willingness to understand all sides of the debate before he landed on a position; it's a great shame we don't have more people like him in public office. We had a good robust debate for an hour, and he came away more across the issues that we faced as a region. Thankfully he went on to be elected to council and enjoyed a successful and universally popular stint as mayor.

The meeting with Dan was a flashpoint for me. As I mentioned earlier, my attitude had been quite belligerent up to this point, and people either agreed with me or they didn't. I didn't really care. And at the other end of the scale, I was probably still ashamed of the way I had kept my head down and shied away from the discussion in the wake of the mine fire. This was a time where we needed to have some brave conversations, and I wasn't prepared to do so.

So rather than working at extreme ends of the spectrum (either unashamedly taking on the coal-fired power industry, or refusing to engage in the conversation), I decided to take a different option: I wanted to understand it.

When someone was outwardly hostile towards me, rather than snap back at them, I stopped and considered what was causing them to feel that way. I reached out to everyone I knew who worked in the power industry or had a deep connection to it. I toured some of the plants and coal mines, and met with friends who were working indirectly in the supply chain. These conversations had a profound impact on me. It gave me an appreciation of the fact that many of these people have worked in the sector for twenty years, and their dads for fifty years. It was more than a job for them, it was their identity, and they didn't appreciate some smartypants from the city telling them coal was a dying industry. But the most important thing I realised was this:

They don't see opportunity coming with the energy transition. They see opportunity leaving.

From that day on, we changed our entire message. We started

posting images on social media of an apprentice collecting their hi-vis uniform, embarking on day one of a new career in renewable energy. We told stories about people like Nick Luke, an eighteen-year-old who did his pre-apprenticeship at Loy Yang Power Station with his dad. He was told, 'Son, I'll give you some work experience. If you want a fifty-year career as an electrician in the valley, you need to get into renewables.'

We told the story of Mitch Richardson, whom I met on my first day in Mirboo North. Richo was our captain and ruckman in the footy team, a big friendly giant with charisma to burn. He worked at the local brewery for minimum wage, and attracted people to the bar on Friday nights just to hear his stories. He was also a refractory worker at Hazelwood Power Station, and spent his days jackhammering concrete and decommissioning plant equipment. Richo had so much to offer, and I invested heavily in him. He started as an installer, went on to become a salesperson, then was promoted to sales manager. He took a career pivot to head up our after-care system maintenance, and eventually obtained his diploma and became the Head of Safety, reporting to our board and across the business on all aspects of OHS and compliance. He more than doubled his salary in the process and went on to build an incredible career without having to leave our hometown of Mirboo North.

There was another unexpected benefit from reaching out to those involved in the power industry. It helped them to understand how I saw the future too. You can imagine how some of them felt about solar power; they saw it as intermittent, unreliable and useless when the sun went down. Baseload electricity had always been king, and the shift to a variable source of electricity seemed preposterous to them. I spent a great deal of time engaged in conversation, explaining how solar with battery storage and smart hot water, combined with software and technology, can help smooth the peaks and troughs of renewable energy supply. Many people I spoke to didn't realise that this transition could be so seamless, they had just adopted the old-fashioned narrative ('when the sun doesn't shine ...') that they had been fed by others. Along the way, I learned about how the electricity grid operates, and how some of their concerns were entirely justified and needed to be addressed.

Rather than a heated discussion about 'coal *versus* renewables', the message was now about appreciating that everyone had a role to play in electricity generation – at least for a few more decades. I started referring to it as the 'energy mix', and explained how, as the percentage of renewable energy increased in the grid, the Latrobe Valley could create the jobs of the future and still retain the jobs we have in traditional generation for a while yet.

This positive message started to land within the local community. And it paved the way for what I consider to be our biggest triumph: convincing Latrobe City Council to install a 100kW system on their head office in 2015. It wasn't the biggest system we had installed at that stage, but it was a statement to the community and it meant a lot to us on so many levels. In the years following, many organisations and environmental groups contacted us, keen to publish our image of the solar panels on the council office, with the chimney stacks of

Hazelwood Power Station clearly visible in the distance. It became the iconic image of the energy transition in the Latrobe Valley. The council even put out a press release, announcing that they were making this move 'to lower their electricity bills'. You can imagine what the comments section on social media looked like!

In 2015, we took another big leap of faith by opening our second showroom and warehouse, in Traralgon. It was one thing to open a shop in our hometown of Mirboo North, in the hills on the fringe of the Latrobe Valley, but it was another to make our first serious investment into the heart of the valley. It was a strong statement that we were here to stay.

We dearly wanted something with a decent size and some highway profile, but we couldn't afford it, and we were sticking with our 'no debt' mantra. We bought something within our financial comfort zone – a small factory with a sneak peek of the highway in the industrial area.

We weren't in a position to stretch ourselves at that point, but there was one shift in the market I had been watching with great interest: the first Tesla electric vehicle (EV) had just hit the road in Australia. From the moment I started looking into it, I knew this would be the key to our success. If EVs became commonplace, they would obviously need to be recharged, and solar companies like ours would become the petrol stations of the future. I rang the sales rep from Tesla and explained my vision, hoping for a good deal to purchase an EV and install a public charging station. I assumed they would be falling over themselves to work with us, but I was told quite bluntly that if I wanted to buy a car and a charging station then I was welcome to. But they wouldn't give me any special favours.

I found an ex-demo Tesla Model S in white, with 4800 kilometres on the clock. It was $210,000, and there was no way we could afford it. Caz strongly advised me not to take the risk, and that we wouldn't be able to afford it for at least a year. She was right, but in a year's time there would be hundreds of them around, and it wouldn't make an impact. I stewed on it for days, and eventually decided to go all in and finance the purchase. Other than the loan from our mortgage, it was our first debt in the history of the business, but it felt right.

We purchased the car, which was one of the very first EVs on the road in Victoria, and had our logo emblazoned on the bonnet, alongside the text:

Tesla Model S – Powered by Renewable Energy

While we were feeling bullish, we pushed ahead with the public charging station and installed it on a powder-coated panel in our front car park, with the sign: 'Tesla EV Charging Station – Powered by Renewable Energy'. It was one of the first free and public EV charging stations in Australia, and we hosted a launch event, strategically timed a few months before the state election. Over 200 people turned up, and every politician and councillor clambered to be photographed with the EV – everyone from the Greens members (who loved it because it was environmentally friendly) to the right-wing Australian Motoring Enthusiast Party (who loved it because it did 0 to 100 in 2.3 seconds). It was very satisfying to have the charging station switched on for the press by the CEO of Latrobe City Council and the Nationals member Darren Chester, who both had right-wing constituents to appease. It proved that EVs could be a unifier and help to accelerate the energy transition in the years ahead.

These days, there are dozens of charging stations installed every week, and the launch of a new site would barely attract a ripple of interest in the media. But back in the very early days, it was big news. The launch event ran as the top story on WIN News that night, attracting tens of thousands of views across traditional channels and social media. Dozens of highly influential people shared the story across their channels, further amplifying the reach. It was also a tremendous free kick for Tesla, especially as we paid for everything ourselves!

Predictably, the story also unleashed a wave of ridicule and scorn on social media about the 'pointless' installation of a charging station in the Latrobe Valley, with people scoffing that no one other than me would be using it for ten years. At the time, I believe there were only two other Tesla EVs in the entire region, so they had a point.

Imagine my surprise when the very next day another Tesla Model S rocked up, owned by the patriarch of the Rijs family, who founded Patties Foods in East Gippsland. He had been driving a Tesla down the Princes Highway to his home (four hours from Melbourne) for a month already, having to stop somewhere and charge off a power point (which took hours). He had been excited to hear about our charger and he leaped out of his car and gave me a big hug, and we posed for a Tesla owners' selfie. I took great pride in posting the image of his car charging on day one and announcing our first customer to the doubters.

Despite a fair amount of push and shove between us and Tesla (mostly due to my tendency to push ahead with a marketing idea before receiving their approval), we went on to build a terrific relationship with them and achieved some amazing things together. We became one of their largest installers of Powerwall home batteries in Australia and installed dozens of EV charging stations on businesses all over the state. In 2018, I was invited to the US for the trip of a lifetime as a guest of Tesla, which was one of the highlights of my career. (More to come on that later.)

We also negotiated a deal with Tesla to include charging stations at no cost on businesses and councils, as a bundle with a solar power system, with Tesla supplying the hardware and subsidising the installation. This was an incredible success, generating hundreds of new customers, and opening a new income stream for the businesses.

The only customer that ever said no to these free charging stations? Latrobe City Council.

Two steps forward, one step back.

Chapter 11

Partnerships

Everyone has their own ideas on the recipe for a successful business. These ideas might change with the economic landscape or as the business strategy (or society itself) evolves. But there are a few elements that remain constant – such as forming strong partnerships. Our long-term collaboration with Tesla is a timely reminder of the importance of partnerships in business.

Without a doubt (and without even factoring in our marriage!), my most important business partnership is with Kelly. This book doesn't even come close to acknowledging the impact that Kel has had on the success of our business, and that's how she prefers it. Kel is an absolute professional in her own right, but she has always been someone who prefers to stay out of the limelight. It's true that opposites attract.

But make no mistake, Kel has been at the heart of every sound decision we have made over the business journey. Whenever I have wrestled with a big issue, or found myself going around in circles and struggling for clarity, Kel has had an uncanny ability to cut through the noise and arrive at the right outcome. Her tendency to think more than she speaks is her superpower. She will often just listen as I rant and rave about something that is troubling me, and when I've got it out of my system, she will say something that is so succinct and on point that it feels obvious from the moment it leaves her mouth.

Kel also has a sixth sense for assessing people and their character, and her ability to ask the right questions and arrive at a conclusion about someone is an immense skill. Within a few minutes, and without saying much, she can usually identify if someone would be a good cultural fit for our business, and if their values are aligned with ours. Kel's radar is rarely wrong and it has led us to make some inspired recruiting decisions over the years.

As our business profile grew and I became known as the 'face' of Gippsland Solar, Kel decided to stay on as a director but to step back from daily involvement, choosing to forge her own career and identity. This has undoubtedly been a positive thing, both for Kel as a professional and for our relationship. She went on to establish herself as a highly respected marketing and communications executive, and we often found ourselves attending the same event, but in our own professional capacities. I have always had a deep respect for Kel's independence, which became abundantly clear on our wedding day when she insisted on replacing the words 'love, honour and obey' with 'two individuals travelling on the same path in life together' in our vows. Every marriage is different and succeeds in its own way, but I believe that Kel's strong identity has been a great complement to my own assertive character, which sets a great example for our three young boys – even if it does result in the odd passionate difference of opinion!

My other most important partnership is with my mum, and, most pleasingly, my dad. Once we had a taste of life in Mirboo North and knew it was everything we'd ever wanted, we decided to build a new home on a one-acre block on the edge of town. Mum and Dad expressed a desire to move here and be closer to support us, which came at the perfect time when we were being pulled in all directions by an increasingly demanding business. After purchasing our old home (with a hefty 'child minders' discount), Mum and Dad also immersed themselves in the Mirboo North community. They joined a number of volunteer groups in town and threw their hand up for any opportunity to spend time with the kids. Mum and Dad managed the after-school and some holiday duties, taking the kids down to the park with their picnic baskets and scooters, or jumping on a bus for a summertime trip to the beach.

Mum has always been incredibly hands-on with the kids (as she was with me), but watching my dad's journey has been heartwarming. He always feels present in a way that I never experienced as a child. It's no surprise that the boys absolutely love their time with Poppy. After feeling like our relationship was unsalvageable at times during my own childhood, I am immensely grateful to have Dad in my life, and for the way he has become a warm and caring presence in my own children's lives.

It's important to know which partnerships you want, but equally to know which you don't want. There was one type of partnership that we had zero interest in – that of a business partner. We made a commitment that we would never take investment or equity (and give up some control of the business) to help us grow. There are plenty of business partnerships that work well and stand the test of time, but, in my experience, many more of them end up falling apart. You might start off with the same mission and values, but people change over time. When the business starts turning a profit, one partner might want to enjoy the benefits and live a comfortable life, and the other might be determined to reinvest everything back in for future growth. Time and again, I have seen businesses that could have achieved incredible success being slowed down by the misalignment between business partners, and it sometimes ends up becoming quite ugly. Kel and I would rather struggle along and navigate the cashflow and growing pains ourselves than take that risk.

It goes without saying that a partnership with your customers is critical to business success, but I have always believed that the partnership with your suppliers is greatly undervalued. I have learned many important lessons from my employers over the years, but one that jarred me heavily occurred early on in my career.

One of my bosses was shouting down the phone at a supplier in a very disrespectful way, trying to squeeze them for an extra discount that they couldn't accommodate. He was seething at them and was completely out of line, from what I could overhear. When he got off the phone, he said to me: 'Never forget this in business, Andy. I work for the customer, and the supplier works for me.' His ruthless approach might work on the odd occasion, but it came back to haunt him when he found himself in a jam.

The very idea of running a business like that seemed ridiculous to me. There will be times when you need a supplier to go above and beyond for you, and they aren't going to bend over backwards to help someone who has made them feel like they aren't valued. Like a marriage, business partnerships (with customers and suppliers) are built on a level of mutual respect.

So many of our competitors would jump between suppliers for a relatively minor saving, looking to save a couple of dollars here and there. We always wanted the best deal possible, but there are far more important things than extracting a couple of per cent on a project. I have partnered with Trina Solar panels for nineteen years (and counting), and Fronius inverters from 2012 onwards. When I had a warranty issue that was a 'grey area' or needed them to look after us in some way, I could lean on these long-term partnerships to get the best outcome for my client. We didn't threaten to take away their business at every opportunity if we couldn't get what we wanted; we would always try to find a way forward. Time after time, this approach has proved to be the right way to build a successful business.

When it comes to customers, the nature of the solar industry is such that sales are very transactional. A customer chooses you to supply their system, they have a good experience with you, but unless they have an issue down the track, that's the end of the relationship. We spent a large amount of time and energy fostering partnerships with customers. In the early years, I would spend two to three days a week driving around to meet our customers after the project was complete, handing over a bottle of wine or a hamper to say thank you. Even just a text message every six months to check in on them is incredibly effective. It's amazing how many times this resulted in a referral of some kind, or at least prompted them to tell everyone they knew about how good their experience was.

You need to turn your customers into advocates and ambassadors, in as many ways as you can. This also meant we had to swallow a lot of unnecessary expense, fixing issues that we were in no way responsible for. Customer service is also a bit like marriage in that respect – sometimes trying to prove you're right is completely unhelpful.

In any partnership, finding ways to create mutual value is the key. Put yourself in the other person's shoes and understand what you can do to make them feel good about themselves, or provide them with value in some way. If it's genuine and authentic, the benefits will naturally flow as a result.

Chapter 12

False Starts

After the successful launch of our showroom in Traralgon, and with the cost of solar fast approaching grid parity, we had a strong sense that we had ridden out the storm, and that Gippsland Solar was set for a period of stable and consistent growth.

We were still putting everything we had back into the business, and cashflow was a constant issue. Kel and I were barely drawing a wage, never feeling comfortable or secure enough to take funds from the business. Admittedly, I was also incredibly tight. I recall one heated argument with Kel about clothes pegs (yes, we'd both had a long day). Our cheap plastic pegs were breaking in the sun, and she wanted to buy these fancy stainless-steel pegs that would last for longer. But they were about ten times the price as regular pegs and I questioned whether we really needed them.

She exploded at me: 'If you're so good at running a business, how come we can't even afford pegs?'

The profits we did make went straight back into expansion. We increased our workforce to around twenty-five employees (including two in-house installation teams) and invested in a handful of vehicles on the road, meaning we now had the structure in place to set us up for sustained success. But in keeping with the theme of our journey so far, another unexpected setback was just around the corner.

Another change in the solar feed-in tariff was announced without warning, dropping it to a measly 5 cents for all new *and* existing systems. At the same time, several negative articles came out around household solar, painting the industry in a poor light. A number of large companies went into administration and left their clients stranded, and there were teething problems in the industry, with an increasing number of customers struggling to get their systems connected to the grid. The combination of these events sent shockwaves through the industry and sales ground to a sudden halt, with warm leads going cold immediately. Even jobs that we had already won were put on hold while customers 'reconsidered their options'. After shedding my conservative nature and making some huge investments into the business, we were pot committed (to use the poker parlance), and this sudden and sharp downturn couldn't have come at a worse time.

I still remember Grant, my operations manager, calling me for a chat at 7am on a Monday morning, and telling me we didn't have many jobs to book in. He sounded rattled.

I asked how many days of work we had for the installers.

'Less than a week.'

I can recall the sick feeling in my stomach, which anyone who has run a business will be able to relate to. My hands were shaking and I broke into a cold sweat. I drove into work and headed upstairs without saying a word, closed the door to my office and stared forlornly at my coffee. A feeling of dread washed over me as I realised that we might have to stand our teams down in the next couple of days, and if things didn't pick up soon, we might have to look at making people redundant. Then I started scrolling aimlessly through the junk folder on my phone. I found an email from the Foster Medical Centre, who had sent an acceptance for a 30kW system (four days of work at that stage) and wanted to know when we could install it. A brief sense of relief turned to panic when I noticed they had sent the email nearly three weeks ago! I frantically called them to apologise and see if they still wanted to go ahead. They thought we had forgotten about them and were about to give the job to someone else, but thankfully they agreed to proceed with us.

The sense of relief was visceral, but temporary.

We scrambled frantically to keep our teams in meaningful work for the next few months, knowing that it would only take a couple of quiet weeks to put us in a vulnerable position. Every day it felt like we were treading water, trying to keep our heads above the surface and take a few breaths. My leadership was tested like I had never experienced before, and I started to crack at the seams. I'm not sure how visible it was to my team, but it had a noticeable impact on my performance as a husband and father. As hard as I tried to leave my professional troubles at the office, I was on the red line, and the smallest thing would set me off at home.

Anyone can be a great leader when times are good. When you're winning jobs and turning a profit, running a business is awesome. You bring a positive energy to everything you do; you can afford to look after your team, and everyone enjoys coming into work. It also tends to flow into your personal life, making you a better person to be around.

But the truly successful leaders are at their best when they are faced with some form of adversity. There are few things more valuable in business than *resilience*. And running a solar business through this period (especially in the Latrobe Valley) was the ultimate test of my resilience.

We called it the 'solar coaster' for a reason. Every day there was something unexpected to contend with. A negative article about solar in the media, which had our customers panicking. A sudden change to rebates or incentives, which had the industry scrambling to ramp up or down and adjust their inventory levels and workforce accordingly. An immediate change in standards or regulation, which was usually announced with little warning, forcing us to put our teams through more training and change our processes.

Suppliers refused to issue credit limits, spooked by this turbulent environment and the amount of solar companies that had come and gone over the past five years. Cashflow was a constant thorn in our side.

And they were just the standard industry challenges.

Overlay that with trying to be an 'agent for change' in a region like the Latrobe Valley in 2015, and those challenges multiplied. Our shopfront was vandalised, I was confronted in the street by people who hated what we stood for, and other businesses were quick to paint us as a 'flash in the pan' success story that would inevitably become a footnote in the history of the region.

In hindsight, the setbacks through this period were incredibly valuable for my own development as a leader. I couldn't run and hide. Everyone was looking to me for a way forward. Over the next few months, I developed techniques and coping mechanisms that enabled me to lead my team with more conviction and positive energy. I stayed up late at night and devoured books and podcasts on effective leadership. I reached out to other leaders whom I held in high regard (including plenty of cold calls), hoping to soak up some insights and wisdom from them. I applied that learning to my behaviours and decision-making, trying to improve my performance under pressure at every opportunity. Self-awareness is the key to leadership, and if you can acknowledge your shortcomings, you will evolve as a leader much more rapidly.

After the initial panic that spread through our business following the announcement, we made a commitment to each other to be calmer and more considered. When these types of changes were dropped on us in the future, we would sit down together and think about how it would change the landscape and how our competitors would be impacted. We would take a day or so to consider all the different angles, and then we would execute quickly and decisively.

By moving at speed and pivoting before other larger (and less flexible) companies were able to, we would increase our share of the overall market every time.

When we encountered any form of resistance in the Latrobe Valley, I used it as fuel to inspire the team: 'Do you know why they're saying this about us? Because we're winning.'

I talked about the importance of courage, and how by succeeding in the face of this adversity, we would leave behind a legacy that everyone could be proud of. The team was fully invested in where we were headed, and I fondly recall the strength of our culture through this formative and testing period.

There were still plenty of days when I felt depleted, and the constant need to dig deep had me drained of energy. There were also plenty of moments when I didn't feel that the Latrobe Valley would ever embrace our vision. I remember coming home from one government roundtable, where the energy minister, Lily D'Ambrosio, came down to meet with local leaders and discuss energy transition opportunities for the valley. The conversation in the room was heated and took a personal tone at times. I slunk out of that room feeling embarrassed at how the region had represented itself and felt like I was wasting my time trying to effect change here. Around this time, I really missed the old days of living in the 'green belt' of Melbourne, where I was surrounded by like-minded people who shared our vision and purpose.

As usual, Kel was my guiding light. After listening to me carry on for a good twenty minutes without saying a word, she put everything into perspective: 'Well, we can move back to Northcote where everyone agrees with us. But if we want to make a genuine impact, then this is where we need to do it.'

On those days when it all felt too hard, or I was worried about something, I often made the mistake of coming into the office and spreading my negative energy. It took me a while to realise that even if I was able to contain my negative thoughts, my body language would tell the real story. I'd never been someone who could put a veneer on and this 'heart on the sleeve' approach had served me well over the years. But I also came to understand how my energy transferred to my team, and there were days when I was far better off staying away from them and dealing with my setbacks in private.

Adversity can either hold you back or propel you to achieve things that you hadn't thought possible. I've always believed that life is very little about what happens to you, and far more about how you respond to it.

Chapter 13

Lift-Off

Once we navigated those critical few weeks in late 2015, commercial work started to flow in and we really started to hit our straps.

This was a pivotal period for the Latrobe Valley. With solar falling in price as grid electricity rose sharply, we had reached the point where installing solar 'just made sense'. Attitudes started to shift, with people and businesses who had previously scoffed at renewable energy starting to recognise the opportunities on the horizon. As our workforce grew and our vehicles became omnipresent on the road, we grew in influence and started to have a seat at the important tables.

Having stepped out of their comfort zone and filled their own rooftops with solar, Latrobe City Council also nominated us for a six-month business mentoring program. Gippsland Solar was selected among eight up-and-coming businesses to take part in the program, which was run by Leigh Crocker from ION Group. I was reluctant to invest too much time into it, and was yet to be convinced that someone with no experience in the solar industry could tell me how to run a solar business.

How wrong I was.

Leigh's approach struck a real chord with me, and he showed me that the principles of business coaching are transferable across businesses of all shapes and sizes. We had a group session to kick off the program, three sessions with just the two of us, and a final group session to summarise our learnings. This mentoring program completely changed the way I thought about the business, and sent us on a completely different (and much more effective) path to success.

Leigh believed firmly that you can't build a successful business without understanding its 'DNA': a set of core values that must guide every decision that you make and every interaction you have. I came to the realisation that it's the only way to successfully scale a business, allowing you to grow your team without succumbing to the temptation of micromanaging them. We developed a one-paragraph statement about the core values of Gippsland Solar and drilled it into our new and existing team members. Whenever we were faced with a pivotal decision on people, strategy, marketing or any other key aspect of the business, we referred back to our core values and questioned whether it was in line with those values. When you look at every decision through that lens, everything in business becomes clearer and you can move forward with purpose.

Leigh also taught me another valuable lesson, and one that I would learn the hard way. It was about how to manage my own energy levels, and not to drift off-course when new opportunities presented themselves.

As a self-confessed energy nerd, the best way I could relate to this approach was to think of my energy levels (my mental and physical capacity) as like having a full 100kWh battery to start every day. You then need to decide how you will spend this 100kWh of energy every day. How many kWh will you spend on the business and on your family? How many kWh will you spend on new ideas or business direction? How many kWh will you spend on developing your people (the old adage of buying them a fish or teaching them to fish)? And most importantly, how many kWh will you spend looking after your physical and mental wellbeing? Every time you take something new on, you need to understand how many kWh of energy that will use up and what to say no to, so you have enough energy to get through the day.

I would have used that system thousands of times over the past ten years. I use it as my 'north star', and it has stopped me from going off on tangents with new business ideas when what I needed to do was focus on nailing down the ideas I already had in flight. When you have ADHD, your mind goes down all kinds of rabbit holes, and it's addictive. It can be a tremendous blessing, but it can also cause you to start and commit to new tasks or projects before you've completed the existing ones. My ASIC register and social media accounts are littered with new business names and ventures. Thanks to this approach, most of those enterprises have never seen the light of day, allowing me to stay focused on the job at hand.

I remember one of these failed ventures clearly. I was at the Intersolar Conference in Europe, and over a few drinks at a networking function, I came up with a business idea for taking care of 'orphaned' solar systems. These are systems that have been installed by a company that is no longer in business, and there are a *lot* of them. We thought it would be great to provide warranty support and help the stranded customer contact the product manufacturers to sort through any issues. The premise made a lot of sense, but as the beer flowed, this business I referred to as 'Orphan Solar' started to develop an energy of its own. We came up with TV ads, and built an entire brand and marketing campaign around this notion of looking after orphaned solar systems (complete with a superhero in a cape). It was a woeful business idea, and in terribly poor taste. But as the night went on and more people jumped into the conversation, we were full of energy (and beer), and convinced ourselves that we were on to something.

I arrived back at the hotel room in the wee small hours, still buzzing from the chat. My recollection of the next few hours is hazy to say the least, but I must have been busy. Imagine my surprise when I arrived back in the office a week later, and sitting on my desk was a pile of documentation awaiting signatures for 'Orphan Solar Pty Ltd', which I had apparently asked my accountant to action. It included the ASIC registration, ABN, options for a logo, draft minutes for the first meeting of the directors and an entire eighty-page constitution for the company. I didn't think this awful business idea would have been a good use of energy, so it all went into the shredder, where it belonged.

I went on to use Leigh's business coaching services for seven years, and the partnership with Leigh took us to places we could never have imagined. Leigh played a fundamental role in our journey, and I enjoy paying forward his lessons to future generations when I have the opportunity.

What followed in 2016 and 2017 was, in a holistic sense, the absolute peak of the Gippsland Solar journey. We had built a strong reputation and surrounded ourselves with an amazing team, and it was an immense pleasure to come to work every day. That era felt a bit like *The Wolf of Wall Street*, with our epic Christmas parties and staff gatherings going down in history. I knew every one of our staff members on a deep level; I knew their families, their pets, everything about them as people. We had a great balance – professional during the day, but more than willing to let our hair down after hours. I couldn't wait to come into work every day, if only to spend time in their company and savour the environment we had created. We opened our house to have the sales team over for poker nights, with ludicrous hats and big cigars the order of the evening. I took great pride in bluffing the up-and-comers in our sales team, showing them that the old dog still had a few tricks. The subculture within our office and installation teams was equally powerful, with regular barbecues and team-building events turning into some very enjoyable sessions. We injected a strong sense of team values into everyone who joined us on the tools. Anyone who couldn't meet that cultural standard was purged from the system, and usually it was organic and mutual.

It didn't take long for us to outgrow the small factory in Traralgon;

in fact, it only took nine months. I was kicking myself that we had taken the safe option and now had to move twice in a year. We needed something six times the size of our current factory, but there was no way we could afford it. I was fortunate that the local representative from Regional Development Victoria had caught wind of our conundrum, and suggested we apply for some financial support from the State Government. We were able to secure a generous amount of assistance, which we had to match dollar-for-dollar. We also needed to create twenty-five new jobs as part of the expansion and were given two years to do this – it only took us six months.

Around this time, we began to appear on the radar of the State Government and other stakeholders in the public service. We were fast becoming one of the larger employers in the Latrobe Valley, and the nature of our business was particularly appealing to them. I built a strong relationship with the energy minister, Lily D'Ambrosio. Politics (and politicians) are always polarising within the community, but I was impressed by her courage to advocate for the energy transition (regardless of her audience and their ideology) and by her personal interest in ensuring that the valley benefited from the opportunities.

While it can be a delicate balance to strike, I've always believed that the private sector needs to have more input into government policy and that it can bring a different perspective that results in better outcomes. It did feel like we were able to have a positive influence on policy and decision-making, but I was always conscious of thinking through an industry lens, and not abusing the trust placed in us by bringing in a personal bias. It takes a long time to establish trust and it can evaporate very quickly if you try to take advantage of it.

In those days, like with my sporting endeavours, I was fiercely competitive in business. I was relentless in my desire to win every job at any cost, and I thought of that as my superpower. Winning a job was a success, losing one was a failure, and I was happy to see my competitors suffering as they struggled to compete with us. This combative approach gave me the energy to 'go into battle' every day, but I can see in hindsight that my ego was spiralling out of control.

I remember talking to a member of the local council around that time, someone I had deep respect for. He had seen one of our social media posts and pulled me aside at a conference for a bit of honest advice:

'Andy, you've built a remarkable business, but you do nothing for the industry. All you focus on is your own success. If you want to be respected, you need to think about how you can work with your competitors.'

I was taken aback by this feedback and dismissed it out of hand. Who was this guy to tell me I should help my competitors out and make them better? If I run a great business and they don't, how is that my problem? I tossed and turned that night, unable to reconcile his comments with my approach, and it nagged away at me for weeks. After spending a large amount of time reflecting on this bigger picture, I reached out to him and asked if we could grab a coffee.

'I get it now. You're saying I should think beyond my own business and focus on how to create a legacy in the industry.'

A broad smile spread across his face. 'Exactly.'

That was another light-bulb moment for me. The one thing that had driven me throughout the years was to make an impact, making the world a better place by accelerating the energy transition. I now understood that my competitors were the same as me: just other people out there trying to make a difference, employ a new apprentice, sponsor their local footy club and put food on the table for their families. If the transition to a net-zero world was the endgame for me, then I needed to see other companies not as competitors but as teammates.

One Saturday, our biggest competitor in Traralgon (who I had openly sparred with for years) rang me sheepishly, asking if I could help him out with some tile feet for a job he was installing around the corner. The wholesalers were closed on the weekend. Andy in 2015 would have taken great joy in sending him packing and making the job take a few extra days, but I took a deep breath and offered to drop the mounting feet off at no cost. He was taken aback by my refreshed outlook and returned the replacement feet the following week, with a hamper to say thanks. We never spoke a harsh word about each other in the market from that point on (at least, I never heard about it), and it opened up a new way of thinking for me, which changed my career direction.

I thought of it as 'co-opetition'.

It wasn't collusion, but rather appreciating that in a disruptive space like the energy transition, we have two obligations. One is to grow our own businesses and put food on the table, and the other is a responsibility to effect positive change. Basically, it's the difference between being a successful business owner and being a champion of industry. Eddy May from NRG Solar is a great mate of mine and one of the sharpest minds I've ever met. He put it all into perspective for me when he said: 'The future of solar is in collaboration.'

Two of my good friends, Jack and Kosta, went on to create an organisation called Solar Cutters, which is built on the premise of co-opetition. For the *Simpsons* fans out there, the name is based on the Stonecutters, which was a secret society with its own membership cards, meetings and handshakes. The first Solar Cutters networking event attracted 400 people, the second one swelled to 750, and it took off from there. What started as a bit of fun between mates became a serious force in the industry overnight. It gave solar companies and installers a unified voice, allowing installers an opportunity to join forces and impact on what we saw as poor policy outcomes, and unconscionable conduct by manufacturers and energy retailers.

Extending an olive branch to our colleagues and competitors over the years has afforded me so much joy and fulfilment, creating business collaborations I never would have thought possible, and allowing me (and them) an unexpected shoulder to cry on when things became too hard.

I still enjoy beating them on a job, though.

I tried everything to find a place where I belonged in my younger days, and my parents thought the discipline of the Scouts would straighten me up a bit. But there were far too many rules for a child of my rebellious nature, so it didn't last long.

My first competitive game of footy, at age 11. That's me with the cowlick hair in the front row. I loved everything about footy, despite having little ability. This was probably one of my last touches of the footy that season!

Every sale of solar hot water was a big deal in the early days, and this was one of my first. The customer was on a main street, so I gave up most of the profit to put an advertising sign on their fence!

Our first business expansion: adding a home office in 2011. With a one-year-old running around the house, it was much quieter to work here than on the kitchen table.

At this point, it was clear we had outgrown our backyard.

I finally convinced Kel to work in the business. It didn't last long, as Kel preferred to embark on her own professional journey – a healthy thing for our relationship, no doubt! – but her marketing mind was an incredible asset along the way.

Our first 100kW system, at the Grand Ridge Brewery in Mirboo North, and one of the first commercial systems in Victoria. Drone images like this are common now, but in 2013 we had to fly a plane over the building to photograph it.

When we installed one of the first public electric vehicle chargers in the Latrobe Valley, early in 2015, people joked that I would be the only customer for ten years. Twenty-four hours later, our first customer turned up, smiling from ear to ear!

Surprising our young superstar Mitch with his first work vehicle. Mitch has come so far since jackhammering concrete at Hazelwood Power Station. Helping to steer his professional journey has been a highlight of my own career.

Few stories within our team had a bigger impact on me than Vince's. His courage in leaving a sales role to follow his dream of becoming an electrician really impressed me, and I was so happy to see him flourish and achieve tremendous things as a result.

Onstage with our first female apprentice, Tracy, at a government panel discussion in the Latrobe Valley. Tracy was a trailblazer for women in renewables, and I loved telling the stories of our team and their journey with us.

My interview with our first Indigenous apprentice, Orson, at a company town hall meeting in 2022. Orson's remarkable journey to become a leader of industry had a huge impact on me. His raw and authentic story that day had some of our team shedding a few tears. A truly inspiring guy.

In the aftermath of the devastating Black Summer bushfires, we donated dozens of off-grid solar and battery systems to restore power to wildlife shelters and emergency relief centres. It was incredibly rewarding work, including this project at the Bat and Roo Wildlife Shelter in Bruthen.

After many years in which my relationship with my parents was strained by my poor behaviour, having Mum and Dad heavily involved in our children's lives has been immensely satisfying.

I was enticed out of footy retirement after a seven-year break. After dishing out plenty of advice to the boys as a coach and umpire, I now had to back it up! The following week was mostly spent in bed recovering.

A rooftop selfie with Victorian State Energy Minister Lily D'Ambrosio. Energy transition requires strong leadership and vision, and the minister has shown that in spades over the years.

We always found time for some fun on our work trips abroad. This one was a cracker.

Arriving at the RACV Christmas Party with Kel in 2019, a few days before the acquisition would be announced. After six of the hardest months of my life spent finalising the deal, this was a moment to be savoured.

Signing off the acquisition of Great Ocean Solar and Electrical with Reece and Nikki (and little Pip in the background!). They were wonderful people with strong values, and it was a pleasure in my new position at RACV to help their business dreams come true.

Jumping on the tools with the team was always my 'happy place', even when we had hundreds of people working for us. It helped me stay connected to the install teams and to understand the daily challenges they face. Even though I slowed them down considerably!

Bringing Gary Ablett Jr onboard as our brand ambassador was a great move: our business boomed in the Geelong area. He was such a warm and humble guy to work with, too.

When it came time to pull the plug, I had a whirlwind of a final week, covering thousands of kilometres by air, land and sea to say thanks to our team.

There were plenty of laughs raised and tears shed that week, and I will miss them dearly.

Kel and me back at our wedding venue fifteen years later, at Toms Cap Winery (now Carrajung Estate) in Gippsland. We've been through a lot together, and it hasn't always been smooth sailing, but I'm forever grateful to have Kel in my life.

After thirteen years of pushing myself to breaking point, travelling with the family on a six-month sabbatical was one of the best times of my life. Kel and the boys sacrificed so much for our business success, so it was lovely to reconnect as a family.

Chapter 14

Putting a Flag in the Ground

The strategy to own the Gippsland region was the key to our success.

It gave us a 'home base', and by entrenching ourselves in the local community, we managed to defend our territory from the well-funded companies from other regions that tried to push into Gippsland. We did some deep analysis on each postcode, understanding the demographics and psyche of each community, and what mattered the most to them. Gippsland is a vast area with a patchwork of different communities that span the entire political and cultural spectrum, so it was no small task.

By this stage, the strategy was working incredibly well and we had developed deep roots throughout the community. If you went to a barbecue and mentioned you were thinking about solar, someone at the gathering would have used us or would know someone in our team. If there was a project being delivered in Gippsland, we were either involved in it or we were aware of it.

One of our competitors joked that there was a force field that kicked in around Pakenham (the gateway between Melbourne and Gippsland), and any time another company tried to quote a job in Gippsland, their car would break down on the highway and their laptops and phones would stop working, like we had somehow scrambled the satellites and cellular network across the whole region. That was a bit of a stretch, but it did feel like we had built an unstoppable momentum.

After years of reinforcing the 'local' message and reinvesting as much as possible back into the Gippsland economy, the rewards were flowing handsomely. It also proved to be a marketing masterstroke. Of all the ways that the large solar companies could try to compete with us, the 'local' message was the hardest for them to overcome. Some of them tried to respond by poaching our people and building a local team, but our culture was virtually impenetrable, so the strategy didn't work.

To reinforce the message, we also created the Gippsland Solar Community Fund, which retained a percentage of sales to support the local region. We started by donating small solar systems to places like Yinnar South Primary School (a tiny school with only thirty students), which had delivered some remarkable projects to champion permaculture gardens and waste management. The one thing they hadn't been able to afford was a solar system, so we installed it at no cost to acknowledge their inspiring leadership. As our sales grew into the millions and then many millions of dollars, we were able to leverage this purchasing power and gain the support of our suppliers, which started matching our donations with their own contributions. This helped us to develop quite the treasure chest, and we were able to sponsor dozens of grassroots clubs and community groups, and donate solar and battery systems to some truly worthy organisations.

The one challenge we hadn't tackled yet was to expand into East Gippsland, which is over 20,000 square kilometres in size – approximately the size of the rest of Gippsland. Being four hours from Melbourne, it has a unique and fiercely passionate identity, and is a hyper-parochial region, where even admitting that you lived in the next town could flag you as 'not local'. They also had a business called East Gippsland Solar, a dominant player that had been around for a long time, and whose name would no doubt create some confusion if we expanded into the market.

We targeted a few specific commercial jobs in the region to gain a foothold, and met a local guy named Landon on a site inspection. Landon was working for another small company that operated from a shed. We formed a partnership with this company, and while working together we found an instant connection. Landon was highly ambitious and found that he was treading water with little growth potential in his current role, so we asked him to come on board to head up our East Gippsland expansion and gave him a sizeable salary bump. It was one of the best decisions we made, as he was someone who was incredibly well respected, and had deep connections across the entire region.

We set Landon a challenge: if he hit $1 million in sales, we'd employ an in-house install team, and if he hit $2 million, we'd invest in a showroom and warehouse on the highway in the main town of Bairnsdale. I figured it would make him hungry for success and buy us a few years before we had to revisit the strategy. I should've expected this, but he hit the $1 million milestone in six months, and the $2 million milestone shortly thereafter, so he tapped me on the shoulder to hold up our end of the bargain. We followed through with those investments, building an exceptional in-house team (several of them coming to us from other local companies that seemed to be struggling with the more competitive landscape).

We also opened a brand-new premises on the Princes Highway, with our grand opening attracting hundreds of people, including the mayor, Joe Rettino, who went on to become a wonderful advocate for Gippsland Solar, and encouraged us to keep doubling down on our investment in the East Gippsland region. Other councillors were also in attendance, along with many business and community leaders. Despite having to umpire the Under 18s football game that morning, the local Nationals MP Tim Bull even made a brief appearance (turning up dressed in his umpiring gear!). It was an incredibly satisfying day, for Landon and for myself, and one of those moments where you pause and reflect on what you have achieved.

With so much momentum behind us, we enjoyed a period of exponential growth in East Gippsland, hitting $10 million in sales within three years, and building a team of twenty local employees in that timeframe. We delivered four of the five largest commercial projects in the region, and most of the largest battery storage projects in East Gippsland. We quickly outgrew our first showroom/warehouse and invested heavily in a custom-built facility in the industrial area to underpin our future growth.

We also created a spin-off of the Gippsland Solar Community Fund for the East Gippsland region, and quickly developed a significant pool of funds to distribute into community projects and donations. We were able to sponsor a number of local groups, and make significant donations towards solar and battery systems for community houses, food banks, shelters and community healthcare facilities in East Gippsland.

The East Gippsland success further reinforced that our business model and strategy was effective. If you want to expand into a new area, you have to throw your heart and soul into it, and make sure you do it in an authentic and genuine way. Employ great people, give back to the community, make sure the local region benefits from your success, and you will earn their trust and support. While many large businesses are seduced by centralisation, cost savings and efficiencies, remote working has reduced the perceived benefits of this strategy. There is no substitute for employing local and reinvesting back into the local community. The further you are from the big cities, the more important and effective this approach is.

Our business was travelling along well, but it was becoming increasingly hard to recruit the talent we needed to deliver quality work. Training up an apprentice takes many years, and due to the sluggish embrace of the renewables industry overall in the Latrobe Valley, there wasn't a pool of experience we could draw on.

We started to explore acquisitions of other businesses to fuel our growth, investing in capability rather than developing it from the ground up. We had been working with a terrific local electrical contractor, WND Electrical, in the Latrobe Valley for a while. Josh and Tim were outstanding tradesmen and had built a great team of half a dozen apprentices. What they didn't enjoy were the other, less visible elements of running a contracting business, such as having to sit in the office every night and complete invoices, compliance paperwork and tax returns. They were starting to move in different directions, so we offered to acquire all elements of their business: infrastructure, customer base, staff – everything except the name and ABN itself. They were more than happy to proceed, but wanted an iron-clad commitment that their team would be employed and supported. We signed the deal, and they all came on board the next week.

It was an outstanding success by any measure. Josh went on to become our Head of Operations in the years ahead, overseeing a team of sixty indirect reports. Tim became our technical guru, designing complex systems and projects and solving issues in the field. He was with us for a number of years, then decided to go back out on his own, rented a small factory from us and continued to deliver our work throughout my tenure. The WND apprentices have all developed into exceptional tradesmen, and have no doubt benefited from the support and structure of a larger organisation. It has provided them with experiences that they would never have thought possible and it's a great example of how acquisitions can be a genuine win-win.

We now found ourselves in a dominant position throughout all six of the Gippsland shires, and had a sense that we had achieved many of the goals we had been striving towards. We walked into every quote, project meeting and tender with an unwavering belief that we were the right company to deliver the job.

This is the point where a new kind of danger started to emerge.

My confidence was soaring and I had started to get ahead of myself. I had always been someone who would ask for feedback from my team, and they knew that when I requested a critique, I didn't want empty platitudes. I wanted something to work on. But as the business became more successful and my profile grew, people seemed afraid to give me the frank and fearless feedback I needed. I was oblivious to this – and that's where having strong relationships with your leadership team is critical.

Grant called me after a team meeting one day when I felt like I had delivered an inspiring speech to my team and really hit the mark.

'Mate, I think you're starting to get a bit out of control. You sounded a bit up yourself today.'

He said he felt like it had been building for a while, and I questioned why no one had told me this when I asked for feedback.

'Because people are intimidated by you.'

That comment hit me right between the eyes. I had always prided myself on being approachable and feeling like I was one of the team. The idea of being intimidating to people around me was confronting.

I once read a quote about confidence that has stayed with me: 'The only difference between confidence and arrogance is whether people like you.'

I certainly nudged the boundaries between confidence and arrogance at times, and my style (which naturally morphs into my team's style) was not always to everyone's liking.

In hindsight, it wasn't helpful that we had enjoyed so much success and a dominant market share in a short period of time. Having a few strong competitors (and losing the odd job) brought out the best in us; it made us innovative, creative and hungry to succeed. With the rise and fall of many of our local competitors, we felt like we had the market tied up and it created a sense of complacency, which can be damaging in business. We had become a big fish in a small pond, and I became a bit 'up myself' as a result.

It was a timely reminder about the value of self-awareness, and how important it is to surround yourself with people who will tell you what you need to hear.

Chapter 15

Storytelling

When times were good, everyone wanted to be a solar company.

We found ourselves competing against 'man in a van' operators, roller shutter companies, telcos, petrochemical companies and incumbent energy retailers with multi-billion-dollar balance sheets. Some of the slicker solar retailers were producing big-budget TV ads with superheroes in capes. Mergers and acquisitions were becoming more common, with large (and well-capitalised) companies willing to try anything to gain a foothold in the burgeoning renewable energy industry.

Compared to these monolithic competitors, we still didn't have much of a marketing budget behind us, and we needed to find a way to cut through.

With our approach to social media starting to gain traction in 2017, we realised this was a critical (and low-cost) way for Gippsland

Solar to differentiate itself in the market. I was prolific on Facebook, Instagram, Twitter and LinkedIn, drafting posts every night once the kids went to bed. And while most of our competitors posted picture after picture of solar panels on roofs, we focused on the people.

We put a deeply personal lens on our content and told stories about our team, our customers and communities, and the students I was mentoring. Social media strategy can be more about drafting and scheduling posts these days, but the most effective content we produced was purely intuitive. Sometimes I would be on a roof with the team, or have an inspiring conversation with a client, and I would have an overwhelming urge to share the story. So I would stop whatever I was doing and post right there on the spot, while I was wrapped up in the emotion and my creativity was flowing.

Social media also became our weapon of choice to combat some of the negativity and tall poppy syndrome that we encountered as we grew our business. In those situations, my impulsive approach to posting came back to haunt me on several occasions and I eventually learned to save a post in my drafts folder and read it again once I had calmed down. We had to deal with competitors creating fake accounts to leave scathing reviews, people we had never done business with complaining about their experience with us, and all the typical negative behaviour that pollutes the social media landscape.

The problem with naming a business after a region is that you leave yourself open to various forms of identity theft. Anyone in Gippsland who installs solar could make a legitimate claim to the name, and we couldn't register Gippsland Solar as a trademark for this reason (which is fair enough). Our competitors pulled out every trick in the book to promote themselves as Gippsland Solar, creating search engine optimisation under the phrase 'Gippsland Solar' (and every variation thereof), running social media posts using our name and attempting to portray themselves as us in any way possible. Three of our local councils even rolled out a solar bulk-buy program (which used a company from outside Gippsland to supply the systems) and called it the Gippsland Solar Bulk Buy. Some customers turned up at the info sessions expecting to find us, and a handful of them actually signed up for a system before realising we were not involved. It created a lot of confusion and anger in the local region. We ran a boosted social media post to pressure the councils to change the program name, with customers jumping into the comments section to vent their frustrations, before we eventually received an apology and it was renamed as the Gippy Bulk Buy. Still smarting at how it had been handled, we ended up running our own local bulk buy alongside this rollout, delivering a hugely successful program of our own.

As we became better known in business circles, we also drew some attention from the big end of town. Every year, the Australian Football League (AFL) has a round which includes the Country Game, played between Geelong and Essendon at the MCG in front of at least 60,000 people. As part of the event, the whole car park is converted into a festival, showcasing businesses from regional Victoria that have a great story to tell.

Imagine my surprise and delight when the AFL rang me a few weeks before the event and asked if Gippsland Solar wanted to set up a marquee and be showcased on the day! After many years of hard work, setbacks and persistence, we were going to one of the biggest sporting stadiums in the world to put our business up in lights. We only had two weeks to arrange a branded marquee, marketing material, staff and other logistics, but we wouldn't have missed it for anything in the world.

What we hadn't realised was that the major sponsor of the Country Game was Powercor, a multi-billion-dollar company that owns the electricity network and infrastructure for the majority of western Victoria, and supplies grid electricity to nearly one million people. With only three days until the game, we were suddenly and mysteriously removed from the event. We had no doubt that Powercor was behind the decision.

Fancy that, our humble solar panel business being seen as a threat to a multi-billion-dollar supplier of grid electricity!

Well, you can imagine what happened next. I took to social media and posted a call to action, headlined 'Gippsland Solar banned from MCG event – by Powercor!' I talked about how proud we were to be chosen to tell our story and how heartbreaking it was to be banned by this multinational corporation on the eve of the event.

I thought the post might gain some traction, but I wasn't prepared for what transpired. Hundreds of people shared it through their network and the post reached nearly 100,000 people within four hours. It was the quintessential David vs Goliath battle. Someone even created the hashtag #shamepowercor, which was shared with great enthusiasm. The comments were scathing.

Later that evening, I received a call from a senior executive, who I have chosen not to name. They sounded like they'd had better days. They apologised profusely for any inconvenience they had caused and said that they would be happy to reinstate Gippsland Solar at the event. And if we would be willing to remove our post from social media immediately, they would greatly appreciate it.

I was quick to accept their apology and invitation, but I left the post up with an edit to say **DECISION OVERTURNED**, and posted a comment to thank Powercor for coming to their senses. I visited their stand at the event and posted a happy picture of us with the Powercor team, which won them a few friends and painted them in a positive light. We have long since buried the hatchet with Powercor and gone on to build a strong working relationship with them. The whole episode demonstrates the tremendous power of social media, giving the little guy a voice that they wouldn't have had a few years earlier.

With all the fear, uncertainty and doubt about the future of the Latrobe Valley, we also found that social media could be a powerful tool to advocate for the region.

In 2017, the Latrobe Valley was shocked to its core when ENGIE, the owners of Hazelwood Power Station, announced it would be closing it down in just four months. Opened in the early 1960s, Hazelwood produced nearly 25 per cent of Victoria's electricity for decades, and in doing so, directly employed around 900 people in the Latrobe Valley. While those in the know understood that the power station was unable to keep operating without an almost complete rebuild, many in the community believed (or perhaps just desperately wanted to believe) that it would continue to operate for a long time into the future. And with unemployment already hovering around 20 per cent in Morwell before the sudden closure, the familiar cloud of coal dust was replaced by a dark cloud of anxiety and hopelessness.

The sense of shock and outrage in the community was palpable. Many of my friends and family were either employed directly by Hazelwood or within the supply chain that relied upon it. One of my best mates had just taken out a sizeable mortgage and found himself without a job three weeks later. Local politicians ran heated campaigns to force the government to reverse the decision, even though Hazelwood had been fully privatised over twenty years earlier. It was purely about economics for the owners of Hazelwood, but it didn't take long before that anger started being projected onto anyone who was in favour of the energy transition.

While being mindful of how sensitive the discussion was for many people, I wasn't going to stay in the shadows and avoid contributing to the conversation like I did after the mine fire. It was a delicate balancing act. It was undoubtedly a positive step forward for the health and wellbeing of the region, and the improvement in air quality would be a tremendous outcome for the community. But I also felt terrible for the workers who had been left blindsided and exposed by the news. Some of the posts by environmental groups and political parties were incredibly distasteful, and showed a complete lack of empathy for those in my home region who were reeling. Imagine finding out that you have lost your job that day, and scrolling through social media to see these green groups triumphantly proclaiming, 'We did it!' with little mention of the workers and their families. These are the moments where the ideological divide between 'right' and 'left' can be driven further apart, undoing much of the progress we have made in building these bridges.

The media focus on the valley was immediate and unrelenting, and, as you can imagine, most of the coverage ran with a narrative that was overtly negative. A group of us involved in the local renewable energy industry were provided with media training, which gave us some valuable insights into how to handle these interviews. The training provider would set you up in front of a camera, with your colleagues watching on from behind the scenes, and after starting gently to soften you up, they would ask a series of questions designed to paint you into a corner. I completely bombed a couple of these attempts and felt my face turning beetroot-red, but at least the embarrassment was contained to a room of like-minded people. It was an invaluable experience and I quickly learned how to stay quick on my feet and avoid going down rabbit holes during these interviews.

As someone who had come to represent the energy transition in the valley, I found myself being interrogated by dozens of reporters from newspapers, radio stations and national TV outlets. What I started to realise was that no matter how they framed the interview when you agreed to it, there was always an angle they wanted to take, and you usually wouldn't find out what that angle was until the interview was live to air.

I had a particularly robust debate with Raf Epstein on ABC

Melbourne, who, after running through the typical platitudes, repeatedly asked me to respond to former prime minister Tony Abbott's comment that Hazelwood should be reopened. After several attempts at producing a 'gotcha moment' from me, I calmly responded with 'Raf, we are a proud region and I'm already seeing the green shoots of what is possible here. It's for others to look in the rear-view mirror. I'm looking out the windscreen at what's ahead.' Eventually he gave up and changed the topic, and I breathed a sigh of relief.

SBS also contacted me and said they were coming to the valley on a 'fact-finding mission' and wanted to tell the story of the Latrobe Valley for their *Insight* TV program. They were reaching out to 'select people who had a story to tell', and they wanted me to join the studio audience with my electrician Adam, a Hazelwood worker we had taken on following the closure of the power station. I was incredibly excited to be a part of it, and to hear that so many other local champions had also been asked to take part.

The filming went for two hours, but the footage would be condensed into a one-hour program. As the camera roamed around the room, we heard from some locals who felt a sense of hopelessness about the future of the valley, but mostly people shared amazing stories about positive ideas and business successes. It was a fascinating and inspiring discussion, and the foyer was full of excited chatter after the show. Like many people, I drove home feeling incredibly proud of how the region had represented itself.

When the show went to air, we were stunned. The overwhelming majority of the discussion they put on air was focused on the doom and gloom, and people who couldn't wait to leave the valley because 'there's no jobs here and we've all had enough'. I felt like it was a pathetic hatchet job, which we should have expected but were still shocked by.

The community outrage was palpable, especially from the people who had been in the room. I'd never seen the Latrobe Valley so unified.

I decided to launch a social media campaign called 'Pump Up Your Valley' to counteract the negativity that was starting to take hold. We committed to telling 100 stories in 100 days, about people and businesses doing amazing things in the Latrobe Valley, and invited nominations from the community. I hadn't thought about the commitment required to run a story every day for three and a half months, including taking photos and writing stories about the nominees, but we were inundated with nominations and could have run the campaign for 200 days (if I'd had the time and energy).

The Latrobe Valley Authority and Latrobe City Council picked up the campaign too, sending a film crew around to interview some of the nominees. It ran several times on local TV, and I spent many weeks travelling around to interview some of the people who had inspired me as I put these stories together. I have no idea how many people the campaign reached, but just the first post (about an inspirational B-Corp organisation called Latrobe Valley Bus Lines, which launched the first hybrid bus in Australia) reached over 60,000 people. That's more than half the population of the entire Latrobe Valley!

Reflecting back on this initiative now, I'd like to think it played a role in shifting the way that the Latrobe Valley thinks and feels about itself, and served as a reminder that our best days are still ahead of us.

Chapter 16

Leaving Home Base

When you're growing a business and you can see where you want to get to, you can remain focused, disciplined and hungry. But as we grew exponentially and became the largest provider in Gippsland, we went from being the hunter to the hunted. We needed a new challenge to keep us on our toes. We needed another mountain to climb.

I mentioned this to Leigh, and his eyes lit up. He'd been expecting this.

'Well, I've got a challenge for you. Can you expand Gippsland Solar out of Gippsland?'

I was hesitant about how the business name would transfer to other regions, concerned that our strength could become a weakness. Coincidentally, one of our biggest competitors had asked me out for lunch that week. After getting through the chest-beating and one-upmanship, he offered me a partnership in his new business venture

151

(on pathetically lopsided terms) to help expand their solar business across Victoria. He sipped the last of his coffee, stood up to shake my hand and finished the meeting with a throwaway line: 'I mean, you guys are hamstrung by the whole Gippsland thing, so clearly you're not going to be able to do it.'

Red flag. Bull. Let's go.

We sat down and wrote a single-page strategy deck over the next few weeks. We went all in and I employed a new right-hand man, a highly experienced general manager who had just been made redundant after the closure of the Hazelwood Power Station. Geoff had led mergers and acquisitions in his previous roles, and managed multinational businesses of the size that we now aspired to be, so we rolled the dice and brought him in.

We planned to target a specific commercial project outside of Gippsland to launch our expansion – something epic that would truly put Gippsland Solar on the map. I had found out about an upcoming tender for Camberwell Grammar School, one of the largest and most prestigious private schools in the country. They wanted to fill the entire campus roof with solar, and to install a battery and EV charger. This would be the largest solar and battery installation on a school in Australia, a project that was eight times bigger than anything we had ever done, and far beyond our technical and financial capabilities. I reached out to the procurement company, which – after conducting its own research to find out what Gippsland Solar actually was – informed me that the providers on the shortlist were 'a little bigger than the Gippsland Solars of the world'.

They were right, but the comment burned inside me for days. I messaged my senior management team the next day and gave them a heads-up: 'We're going for this job. And we're going to win it.'

Grant pointed out that we wouldn't even know where to start on quoting and delivering a project like this, but I decided to worry about that later.

I hustled like I'd never hustled before to secure that job. I tracked down all the key decision-makers at the school and sought letters of support from our suppliers stating that we were worthy of bidding on such a prestigious project. Eventually they relented and invited us to tender for the project.

I brought in another installer, Brendan, who was rough around the edges but one of the smartest guys I've ever met. Brendan had been raving about the latest technology for commercial projects, using a specialised drone to build a complete 3D model of the site. It would fly over the school on autopilot, then load hundreds of images into a software program and stitch them together, constructing an interactive model to measure the shading impact of any surrounding objects. With this model, we could measure the specific impact of tree shading or plant equipment on the roof, and give the customer an exact report on how much solar electricity the system would generate per year. You could even increase the height of a tree that was still growing and measure the shading impact in ten years' time. Today, this technology is quite commonplace across the industry, but it was way ahead of its time back in 2017.

We kept this innovative secret weapon in our back pocket for the presentation. I knew most of our competitors well from years of crossing swords. They included huge incumbent energy retailers, construction companies that delivered Australia-wide rollouts for government and councils, and specialist commercial providers that turned over tens of millions of dollars every year. I was confident that I knew what their sales pitch would be: they would go in and dazzle the client with slide after slide of epic commercial projects, and throw huge numbers around about the size of their pipeline, their balance sheet and how they were the only provider worthy of delivering a prestigious project like this.

We asked to go in last. The boardroom was as breathtaking as it was intimidating, steeped in history and stunningly finished off with mahogany furniture. The whole management team of Camberwell Grammar School was sitting on the other side of the table, along with four people from the procurement company, all impeccably dressed. From our team, it was just me, Geoff and Brendan in our polo shirts, with a backpack slung over Brendan's shoulder. For those familiar with the classic Australian movie *The Castle*, there was a Dennis Denuto energy about the whole scene, but I didn't think relying on 'the vibe' would be enough to secure this job.

We jumped into our presentation, which covered all the usual elements of the project, showing them that we had thought of every technical and safety aspect. You could tell from the gentle nodding and lack of response that this had all been covered by the other companies.

I took a deep breath before the grand finale.

'Now, I'm going to conclude our presentation with something that I don't believe has been done before in our industry.'

I turned off the lights in the room for effect. Brendan logged into the 3D drone modelling program, and, using his mouse, panned around a replicated model of the entire school. There was a collective gasp of breath and plenty of gazes exchanged around the room. It was a sure sign that we had made an impact.

I closed the laptop, and they all sat there without saying a word.

'Gentlemen, this is why Gippsland Solar is the worthy company to deliver this project. We might not be as big as the other companies, but it means more to us.'

It landed exactly as I had hoped.

They asked us to bring the drone model up again, the room full of excited chatter and plenty of detailed questions.

Brendan jumped in. 'I've actually got the drone here in my backpack if you're interested.'

'Oh yes! We're interested!'

He pulled the drone out and fired it up, and they gathered around it like kids in a candy store. They were absolutely fascinated by it. After half an hour, we thanked them and left the room, knowing we had given it our best shot.

The guy from the procurement company rang me two days later. He informed me that our price was higher, we didn't have as much relevant experience and there was a question as to whether we had the financial bandwidth to deliver the project.

But the board was unanimous. They wanted to go ahead with the Gippy guys.

I took a deep breath, quietly thanked them for the opportunity and hung up. I stared at the phone for a while, unable to comprehend what we had just pulled off. Then I rang Grant.

'We've won the Camberwell job, mate. We're off to Melbourne.'

Despite being way out of our depth, we nailed that project. The team made a commitment to stay away from home, living around the corner until the job was done. We developed a handful of industry-firsts, including wireless comms between buildings, and building customised smartphone apps to control the system remotely. We even designed a complete off-grid classroom, disconnecting two science classrooms from the grid and installing separate solar and battery systems, with a TV monitor in each room to show their electricity consumption. We folded that project into the curriculum, with the students competing on energy efficiency throughout the school year.

Walking around the roof with my team at the end of the job was a surreal experience. I was bursting with pride at what we had achieved, as satisfied as I've ever been in business.

The project positioned Camberwell Grammar School as the pre-eminent school in Australia with regard to sustainability, and I have no doubt that it elevated their reputation. Projects like this hadn't been done before at the time, so the social media post afterwards went viral, reaching over 90,000 people and being shared by politicians and business leaders from around the world. We brought dozens of clients to the school for a site walk in the years ahead, showing them firsthand how we had managed a project of that size and complexity.

We also returned to the school several months later with our friends at Tesla, bringing a few EVs and a Tesla Tiny House along with us. We hosted a Sustainability Day for the school, holding a special assembly to explain the benefits of this project to students and teachers, and how groundbreaking it had been in the renewable energy sector.

And, of course, I brought out the drone again. The kids went crazy.

We ran at a significant loss on the Camberwell project. We sank everything we had into building our IP, purchasing software and hardware, including extra features at our own cost, and, as usual, we threw a large amount into marketing. As a result of that strategy, the 2017 financial year was the only time that Gippsland Solar posted a (slight) financial loss, but we saw the Camberwell project as an opportunity to establish ourselves in the private school sector. We went on to dominate the space for years, winning a lion's share of the largest and most prestigious private school jobs in Victoria. The competitive nature of private schools certainly helped, and after installing an even larger system for their 'competitor', we would contact the school to let them know that their record had been broken. They would invariably want to add another 50 or 100kW to reclaim their title, and on it went!

After the success of Camberwell Grammar, we offered to acquire Brendan's business in the same way we had with Tim and Josh. His team of eighteen employees came on board with him, and despite some ups and downs, it also turned out to be a great success. Several of them went on to become senior managers or team leaders with us in the years ahead, and others branched out and started their own successful electrical businesses.

We had now added a Melbourne team to our workforce, and started to become a force to be reckoned with beyond Gippsland. It did bother some people that we weren't 'local', in the same way that we didn't want out-of-town providers coming to Gippsland in the early days, so we made sure to employ a local team or contractors wherever we went. I remember quoting a commercial job in Bendigo one day, and the client said, 'I don't know how I feel about you blokes from Gippsland taking business from a local Bendigo company.' After focusing on how we employ local people, I decided to try another angle.

'There's a handful of Bendigo Banks in Gippsland. Why shouldn't there be a Gippsland Solar in Bendigo?'

He laughed, and we won the job.

Chapter 17

My People

By early 2018, the business had grown significantly, and as a result our workforce increased exponentially.

Despite a few tales of regret, we had been incredibly fortunate with the calibre of people we had assembled. By this stage, like many businesses in a small town, our workforce was still largely made up of my friends and family, including Kel, Mum, Dad, my footy captain, cricket captain, and a bunch of mates from Mirboo North that we had invested in from the ground up. Grant was the coach of the Under 18s in Yarram, so we ended up with half of his footy team on the tools. I'm sure he would have thrown in an apprenticeship with Gippsland Solar to entice them across from rival clubs!

Up to this point, employing friends and family had been a fantastic boost to our culture. Whenever you walked into one of our offices or warehouses, there was a powerful energy that was hard to describe.

Everyone was so deeply connected to the vision we had set out, and to each other, and it made coming into work an absolute pleasure. It was the simple things I appreciated. I would arrive at the office on someone's birthday and see the staffroom already decked out with streamers, balloons and a cake. If it was for an installer, we would arrange an early finish for them so we could sing 'Happy Birthday'.

The depth of our culture was also our greatest strength during the darkest times. One of my friends, Todd, worked for us for a few years in a number of sales and admin roles. We also played footy and cricket together, and his wife played netball with Kel. Our professional and personal lives were completely intertwined.

One afternoon in February, Todd's wife was tragically killed in a car accident, and it shook the entire business to its core. Everyone drifted aimlessly around the office for many weeks, unable to come to terms with this tragedy. On a personal level, the hardest part was having to step up and lead my team through the grieving period, while also taking time to support my mate and look after my own health and wellbeing.

I posted the details of her funeral in our team chat and didn't get much of a response. But when I arrived on the day, I was stunned to see that every single one of Todd's workmates had made the effort to attend. Some of them had driven three to four hours to be there, but they made a commitment as a group to turn up and show their support. Knowing that they had taken this upon themselves without any input from me was incredibly powerful, and I felt no shame in shedding a few tears while addressing them over a team dinner that night. It was the proudest moment that Kel and I had experienced on our business journey, seeing that the culture was now driving itself by supporting a much-loved colleague during a period of unimaginable grief.

I believe that what defines an exceptional culture is not your best handful of performers, but your worst handful. Every business will have superstars who are great contributors to the fabric of your organisation, but a few bad eggs will have far more impact. When you have identified that someone is damaging your culture, you need to address it immediately, and if you aren't able to turn them around, you need to be decisive and act swiftly. Sometimes they will be your higher-performing salespeople, your most knowledgeable or talented installer, or someone whose departure will have an immediate and significant impact on business performance. But if you are concerned about the cost of acting, take a moment to consider the cost of *not* acting.

We had the same ups and downs as any workforce while we grew. Sometimes my judgement was poor and I made some bad calls. Like many businesses, over the years we employed some people whose values and behaviours were completely misaligned with our own. We had good employees lose their way, drop their standards and become damaging to the culture, and learning how to recognise the warning signs and act on them was a constant challenge.

It became increasingly difficult as the size of our team grew. In our formative years, I was connected to every decision and I could exercise my judgement based on my firsthand experience. When you have a large workforce, there are hundreds of decisions and judgement calls being made every week. It's not possible to be across every one of those decisions, so you have to put the right leaders in place and trust them to do the right thing by the business. Almost every piece of information you receive as a leader will have some colour or bias to it. The key to good leadership is learning how to process many different opinions and look beyond that bias (including your own) to make the best judgement call.

There were also plenty of times when I handled situations poorly. More often than not, it was a result of reacting too quickly, instead of waiting for my emotions to settle down. When you make those errors of judgement, it's important to acknowledge it and be humble enough to admit that you were wrong. Much like parenting, it sets a valuable example for your team in how to take responsibility for your actions.

Leading people can place you under a great deal of strain and pressure, but it's also a tremendous privilege. And when you invest in someone and watch them flourish, there are few things that feel more satisfying.

It's impossible to overstate how important having a meaningful job can be in improving someone's life. I have always had the deepest admiration and respect for those who have come from a challenging upbringing, yet were able to break the generational cycle with a combination of our support and their own determination. As someone who didn't have a promising start to life himself, I was drawn to (particularly young) people who I felt had something more to offer the world than what they had shown thus far. When you believe in someone and invest in them on a personal level, it's amazing how often their confidence soars and they go on to achieve exceptional things.

Some of these stories have had a huge impact on me, and on the industry more broadly.

Orson was our first Indigenous Australian to sign up for an electrical apprenticeship, at a time when there weren't many First Nations people in the solar industry. He had been raised by his aunty in East Gippsland and had dealt with a few challenges in his life, but was highly influential among young Indigenous kids (largely due to his sporting prowess). His first week was a huge step out of his comfort zone, and he had a panic attack while travelling away for a commercial install. He wanted to come home and throw it in, but we convinced him to stay the night. He felt better the next day and developed a strong connection with his colleagues throughout the week. Orson went on to achieve incredible things with us, completing his apprenticeship and becoming a team leader. He has settled down with his partner, Phoebe, in Bairnsdale, bought a house and welcomed their first son, Jahkarri, to the world.

Orson has become a trailblazer for his community, bringing two more Indigenous apprentices under his wing and guiding them on their journey. He also travels around the state to chat with Indigenous groups, mentoring and encouraging others to take up a career in renewable energy. Despite being shy, Orson agreed to a one-on-one interview with me onstage at our staff party one year, and his raw and authentic story left our team speechless and emotional. Orson went on to become one of the ten faces of 'Careers for Net Zero' in a national campaign, becoming one of the country's foremost leaders in this space. He has been on a wonderful journey.

When it comes to people, it's hard to overstate the importance of powerful storytelling. Over the first years, whenever we advertised for apprentices, we could never attract female applicants. I remember the day our first female apprentice, Tracey, joined our Latrobe Valley team. She fitted in perfectly from day one. We felt that Tracey would be a tremendous role model for other aspiring female tradespeople, so we told her story and posted it across our social media channels. Tracey's story resonated with Kayla, another young woman in Traralgon who had grown up on a farm, who loved the outdoors and had always wanted to do a trade of some kind. But with few apparent pathways for female tradespeople in the valley, she didn't know where to start looking. Kayla was inspired by Tracey's story, reached out to us for a chat and started with us the following week. Kayla also went on to become a star, forging a pathway for even more women to join our installation teams in the years to come.

To highlight how far we still had to go as an industry, when Kayla became pregnant in the third year of her apprenticeship and we contacted her training provider and asked what the process was for deferring and completing her qualification, it was immediately apparent that they had never had this issue before and didn't know how to handle it. Considering half the population are women, it's quite staggering that this was unchartered territory for the sector.

Sometimes these success stories spring up from places you don't expect. Vince was a friend in whom I had always seen something special; there was a warmth about him that lit up the room. He was whip-smart and humble yet incredibly charismatic. With a stroke of his handlebar moustache, Vince could tell a story like few people I'd met. He was born to work in sales.

I offered Vince a role in the sales team and spent many hours shaping and moulding him. But after jumping out of the blocks and enjoying early success, he struggled to find his groove, which slowly but surely chipped away at his confidence and made him feel increasingly miserable. We could both sense it, but I'd invested heavily and desperately wanted him to succeed, so I avoided having the uncomfortable conversation.

Twelve months later, having just settled down and taken on a significant mortgage with his partner, Vince addressed the elephant in the room. He came to me and cut straight to the chase: 'Andy, I just can't do it. I'm sorry to let you down.'

I could see the feeling of defeat in his eyes.

Rather than throwing in the towel entirely, Vince expressed his burning desire to become an electrician. In his time with us, he had developed a passion for renewables, but had fallen out of love with sales. He wanted to spend his days outdoors with the teams, working with his hands and helping to solve problems. I explained to him that this was a big gamble: moving from a sales wage to a mature-age apprenticeship would be a huge step backward, and he would face a significant learning curve. The pressure of keeping ahead of a mortgage, combined with the extra schooling required, would be a big risk at a time when he was feeling a bit lost in life. I wasn't sure that he had what it took, but Vince was convinced he could do it.

The rest is history. Vince threw himself headfirst into his apprenticeship, immersing himself in the role and building his knowledge of data and communications after hours. He became our go-to guy for technical problems, becoming highly respected by his (far more experienced) peers. He also retained his flair for customer service that I had been drawn to, and could settle down the most irate customer with his warm and gentle nature. He aced his studies and went on to become one of the great stories within our business.

Finding a way to get the best out of people goes far beyond understanding their job. You need to understand them as people: what motivates them, what they deal with in their personal lives, what their dreams and aspirations are. I strongly believe that your employees are not just names on a payroll, they are people with a story to tell.

The People and Culture department was the last role I was willing to hand over. Holding on to it tightly while also managing myriad other business pressures created an increasing weight on my shoulders. I felt all my team's highs and lows personally, which was becoming unsustainable as the size of the team grew.

I thrived on this pressure for many years, but I was about to learn that everyone has their limits.

Chapter 18

What Goes Up ...

Kel and I had made a pact that no matter how much the business grew, or how busy our professional lives were, we would always put family first. But as Gippsland Solar grew in size and influence, I found the work–life balance harder and harder to manage.

By 2018, our three boys were getting to the age of competitive sport, which was something I had been looking forward to since they were born. I ran the Auskick program on Friday afternoons for six years. I coached their footy team in the winter and their cricket team in the summer. Every spare moment was spent umpiring, washing uniforms, discussing logistics with opposition coaches, ferrying kids around (not just my own), and helping them find their lost footy boots, cricket whites or mouthguards. By the time all three boys reached the competitive sports age, they were collectively playing around 150 games of cricket, footy, tennis and basketball every year, and I only missed a handful of them.

I also started receiving invitations to travel across the globe for conferences and factory tours. Over the next few years, I made business trips to Europe (four times), and visited factories and met suppliers in the USA (twice), Korea, China, Thailand, the Middle East and Singapore. I've taken over a beer garden with colleagues in Munich, drank soju and sang 'Gangnam Style' in a karaoke bar until 5am in Seoul, stumbled across an epic underground nightclub in Shanghai, and survived a trip to Vegas that took about ten years off my life.

The highlight was an invitation to tick off the number one item on my bucket list: a trip with a bunch of my closest industry friends and colleagues to a global Tesla conference in Reno, Nevada. We also toured the Tesla Gigafactory in Nevada, and the Tesla EV manufacturing facility in Fremont. We drove a new Model 3 (which wasn't available in Australia at this point) around the desert, and had our minds blown at the sight of a fully automated EV factory producing around 2000 cars per day. We watched one robot weld the chassis, hand it to another robot to complete their job, and so on until the process was complete. The whole two-week experience can only be described as surreal, and my feet barely touched the ground on that trip. I reflected on those early days when we had purchased one of the first electric vehicles in Australia, and people had scoffed at the idea of installing a public EV charging station. Fast-forward only three years and the scale of what was unfolding was something that no one had ever imagined. It felt like we were right in the middle of a revolution and that the vision we had all those years ago was becoming a reality.

To add the cherry on top of this incredible trip, I was invited to take up a guest-speaking role at the conference, sharing the story of Gippsland Solar with hundreds of Tesla's largest partners from around the world. As someone who was terrified of public speaking, with my first attempt in 2008 turning into an unmitigated disaster, I had knocked back these types of invitations in the past. But having slowly built up my confidence in front of familiar audiences and small community groups in Gippsland, I was starting to not only endure these speaking engagements, but to also enjoy them. This would be on another level entirely and I wasn't going to let the opportunity slip by.

The Tesla team had one demand, and it was non-negotiable: 'Andy, we know how much you love your social media. But there cannot be any posting about this event, under any circumstances. It's strictly under wraps.'

As someone who had had the odd run-in with Tesla around marketing and communications, I knew that when they said something was under wraps, they meant it. But they also knew me well by this stage, and when I nodded feebly and agreed not to put any posts up, they must have known I couldn't be trusted.

I've never been one to prepare detailed slide decks, and on the day of the talk, I found myself going on tangents and retelling stories that just felt right based on the energy I was getting from the audience. I honestly couldn't tell you what I spoke about for fifteen minutes, but I remember the crowd laughing, and judging by their response at the end, the presentation landed well. It also included a few tongue-in-cheek remarks about how much Australians hate the 'big bully energy retailers', unknowingly firing a shot across the bow of the presenter from one of these retailers, who happened to be up next!

True to form, I decided to go with my standard approach of asking for forgiveness, not permission, and drafted something up for social media. I asked my friend to take some pictures of me at the lectern in front of the Tesla branding to accompany the post. The Tesla team were watching me and my LinkedIn feed like a hawk all day, sensing the inevitable act of insubordination. But I waited until everyone was at the conference dinner that night. As soon as the main meal hit the table, I published the post on my channels and watched the reactions roll in. By that stage, I had built a network of around 12,000 followers and connections on LinkedIn, so it had hundreds of likes and reached thousands of people within thirty minutes. As I was tucking into my dessert, I saw a couple of people from the Tesla team striding towards me in a purposeful way. One of them had a phone in his hand, and they didn't look impressed.

I flashed them a smile. 'All right, guys, you're on to me. I'll pull the post down.'

I don't think they saw the funny side.

Afterwards, I started receiving more of these guest-speaking roles from Europe and Asia. I was also asked to contribute to podcasts, speak at government and council roundtables, and work with start-ups and aspiring entrepreneurs from around Australia and the world. Australia is a very interesting market to the rest of the world, having the highest penetration of rooftop solar per capita in the world.

I think people were also fascinated by our story of starting Gippsland Solar in the heart of coal country, and having to build social licence while also building our business. We had become a microcosm of the energy transition, providing some green shoots in a region where some people felt the 'glory days' were over. After years of feeling that we had picked the worst place in Australia to start our renewable energy business, it became one of our greatest strengths.

I found myself contributing to documentaries about the energy transition, the aftermath of the Hazelwood closure and the inevitable shift to a net-zero world. The highlight was being featured in a global documentary called *Carbon – The Unauthorised Biography*, alongside the incredible Sarah Snook, an Emmy Award and Golden Globe winner for her role in the TV series *Succession*. It was produced by Genepool Productions, which had also won Emmy Awards for its previous work. My role was to wrap up the documentary by talking about my positive vision for the future (particularly in the Latrobe Valley), and it took a lot more time to film than I had expected. There were some very early starts and long filming days, such was their fastidious attention to the smallest details. The cinematography was absolutely stunning, and *Carbon* went on to win a whole swag of film and TV awards from around the world.

By now, you're probably thinking that my life seems to be travelling along quite nicely. Kel and I are in our mid-thirties, happily married with three young kids who are in school during the week and loving their sport on the weekends. Business is booming, we've built a terrific team and we're no longer living 'hand to mouth' with our cashflow and business performance. After years of hard work, we are entering a stage of life where we can relax and enjoy the benefits.

But the pressure of having all these responsibilities and still having to lead a growing team was becoming suffocating. My phone didn't stop pinging and it felt like someone always needed me. I had little regard for self-care, seeing it as optional, something that could wait until I had the time. I was dismissive of mindfulness or meditation. I was exercising and running long distances regularly, but it was more to push my body so that I didn't have the energy to think about my issues. I hadn't taken a genuine break in ten years.

I responded in the same way I had to previous challenges – by running faster and trying to do it all. I said yes to everything, professionally and personally, and the only way to manage these moving parts was to keep hustling, stay up late working, wake up early and go again. This had been going on for years, and was yet to catch up with me.

Something had to give.

Chapter 19

... Must Come Down

As a passionate multitasker with ADHD, I preferred life to move at a frantic pace.

Gippsland Solar had grown to seventy staff seemingly overnight, and we now had teams spread out all over the country.

Kel's own career was flourishing outside of the business too. She had joined the marketing and communications team at Destination Gippsland, the regional tourism board. It was Kel's dream job, and with her limited spare time, she had signed up for a Master of Marketing with Monash Business School. After many months of long nights and weekends, she completed her Master's with a Dean's Honour, scoring in the top 2 per cent of the school. Considering most of her classmates were studying full-time, it was an incredible effort, and another reminder that I am well out of my intellectual depth!

With all of this going on, Kel and I were passing each other like ships in the night. Every other day, someone was away for work or had an evening meeting. Looking back, it felt like we were moving faster and stretching ourselves thinner every day, and it had to snap back eventually.

With my next work trip to Europe looming in June 2018, the business becoming more self-sufficient and Kel's studies complete, we decided to head over as a family and turn it into a month-long holiday.

It was exactly what we needed. We spent a few weeks soaking up the European summer and I could feel my stresses melting away with each passing day, just spending quality time together as a family. I'd always been a hands-on dad, and it dawned on me that over the past few years, I had stopped taking the time to read a book, complete jigsaws or kick the footy with the boys after work.

The last leg of the trip was in Barcelona, and we spent the final day of the holiday floating in the pool. After dinner, we put the kids to bed, Kel went for a walk, and I relaxed with a beer and watched the World Cup final. I'd been so disconnected from work, I hadn't given a moment's thought to what I would have to deal with when we arrived back home.

On the TV, the final whistle blew to signify the end of the game, and it was like a snap back into reality.

'Right, that's it. Holiday's over.'

After years of running on the hamster wheel, I had finally had some time to let my mind relax and that was when it all started to unravel.

I started thinking of all the things I would have to deal with back at work. The unresolved staffing issues. The angry customer refusing to pay their bill.

'What if we have cashflow problems?'

'What happens if we don't have enough work on?'

'How will the kids deal with Dad not being around as much again?'

It went on and on inside my head. I glanced at the clock. 1.30am.

It started with a twitch in my left hand. Faint at first, then noticeable and uncontrollable. Then my right hand followed suit.

I got up and started pacing, went into the spare bedroom, and next thing I was lying on the floor in a pool of sweat. What followed was a complete physical and emotional breakdown, which left me curled up in a ball as waves of emotion and physical pain washed over me.

My first panic attack.

The pain eventually eased off a bit. Although it was the middle of the night in a foreign location, all I could think to do was flee the hotel room and just run. I ran until my legs hurt and my heart felt like it was going to burst out of my chest. Back at the hotel, I collapsed in a heap and passed out through utter exhaustion. I woke up the next morning after a few hours of sleep, feeling like I'd been hit by a bus. 'What the hell was that all about?' I thought to myself.

I staggered down the stairs and was greeted by the chaos of a family in full packing mode. I didn't say anything to Kel and just stared forlornly at my cereal bowl, feeling the cornflakes swirling around inside my belly.

Our chaotic flight schedule home to Australia was the last thing I needed in my rattled state of mind. We were due to arrive in Dubai at 4pm, check into a hotel for seven hours, take a quick nap, then wake up at 11.30pm for a 2am flight back to Melbourne. I couldn't sleep on the first leg of the flight, but despite being utterly exhausted, I then lay in the hotel bed for four hours, staring up at the roof and feeling my heart rate increasing and decreasing at regular intervals. I had another sleepless leg of the flight back to Melbourne, this time for fourteen hours, and by the time I got back into my own bed, I was a wreck, having been awake for the best part of three days.

As anyone who has experienced a panic attack will know all too well, the first one is the most terrifying. You have no idea what's happening, but you know it's bad, and there's a fleeting moment where you think you might die. It's awful beyond words.

Unfortunately, that feeling was about to become all too familiar. Despite coming home and finding that the business was running well and my worries were unfounded, I had another panic attack in the week after we returned. Then another the following week. Then again two days later. The panic attacks were increasing in both frequency and intensity. It usually happened when my head hit the pillow. Once you think to yourself, 'I hope I have a good sleep tonight,' that's it. You've lost the battle.

The only way I could shake these crippling attacks, day or night, was to throw my sneakers on and run, until I couldn't run any further.

It was the peak of winter in Gippsland, but I would still jump out of bed and belt around the streets of Mirboo North at all hours.

Literally trying to run from my troubles. One night I ended up at the golf course at 1am, running lap after lap, uphill and downhill. It was absolutely freezing, my fingers were numb, and I was getting belted by the wind and rain. Eventually I couldn't lift my legs any longer and just collapsed. I tripped and fell, lying face down on the 15th fairway and shaking like a leaf from sheer exhaustion, soaked from head to toe in a combination of raindrops and sweat. I lay there for a long time and eventually trudged back home, ashamed and deflated, wondering if this horrible feeling was going to be with me forever.

For the next few weeks, I suffered wave after wave of these episodes. I was so tired that my whole body felt numb. The stomach cramps were crippling to the point where I had to curl up in the foetal position on the floor. Unsurprisingly, it brought on a serious bout of anxiety and left me feeling depressed and helpless. I'd always considered myself to be a positive and upbeat person who was able to take things in my stride, but suddenly I found myself absolutely broken, regularly bursting into tears and unable to pull myself back together.

I sought solace in making regular (and increasingly desperate) calls to Beyond Blue, the national mental health hotline. I was incredibly grateful that they were available twenty-four hours a day. You can't pick and choose when another episode will happen. When these panic attacks washed over me in the middle of the night, I couldn't wait until the morning to speak to someone. When you're in that headspace at 1am, even 2am feels too far away.

The thing I didn't understand was that, on paper, life had never been better. I could think of many other times in our journey when things had been harder. To the outside world, it looked like I had everything. But inside, I was falling apart.

Just as I was starting to get things back under control, news came through that a mate of ours had gone missing overseas. Eventually his car was found near a clifftop and we were devastated to hear that he had taken his own life. He was in his mid-twenties, a star footballer and one of the happiest blokes I had ever met. His infectious smile went from ear to ear. Everyone loved him and we felt like our heart had been ripped from our collective chest. It was deeply uncomfortable to know that someone at his stage in life, with the world seemingly at his feet, could have made this decision, and the news came at a time when I was already extremely fragile.

It could have gone either way for me at that stage, but the terrible news shocked me into turning things around. I saw the impact that his loss had on his friends and family, with many of them completely unaware that he was battling his inner demons. It's hard to admit, but in my darkest times, when I felt that there was no way out of the prison inside my head, my mind went to some awful places. For those who haven't experienced depression and anxiety, it's the feeling of hopelessness that does the most damage. When you're in the middle of an episode, or suffering from them repeatedly, it feels like things will never be okay again.

During this period, I withdrew and wandered through life like a ghost, completely devoid of any feeling and unable to communicate with people. I used to love the early-morning trip to our local cafe, spending the first thirty minutes of every day immersing myself in conversation with whoever was there. Now I made my coffee at home, or ordered it online so I could quickly pop in and out without having to engage with anyone. As a card-carrying extrovert who loves being around people, it was strange to find myself crossing the street to avoid having conversations.

At this stage, my ambition had completely diminished. In my early teens, when I was bullied relentlessly, all I ever wanted was to have a solid group of mates who I could feel comfortable with. Over time, I started to become that person I had wanted to be, and my ambition became greater. By 2018, it had grown to such an extent that nothing short of changing the world would have been sufficient. And now here I was, a frail and broken soul, whose only ambition was to sleep five hours a night without waking up in a pool of sweat.

As you can well imagine, this downward spiral had a profound impact on my ability to perform my duties as a husband and father. The kids were visibly worried about me. I tried to keep a brave face, but they were acutely aware that something serious was going on with Dad. One day my youngest boy, Charlie, walked up to me cautiously, paused and placed a hand on my shoulder.

'Are you okay, Dad?'

Kel was an absolute powerhouse through this time, shouldering the extra load and trying to ease the pressure on me. If it impacted on her own wellbeing at the time, she did a remarkable job of not letting it show.

And, of course, it also had a significant impact on my team at work. I went missing without notice, I failed to turn up to meetings and I started rejecting speaking and presentation gigs that I would have given anything for a little while ago. I was too depleted to explain to my team what was happening to me, so I just withdrew from life and business. It must have been worrying for them too.

It's these flashpoints that teach you the most important lessons. This period of absence made me realise that our business didn't have solid foundations. We had few systems and processes in place, and when I wasn't around to get involved in decisions, they got stuck in a bottleneck. I had terrific leaders around me, but I hadn't empowered them. Whether it was my passion, micromanaging nature or just plain ego, I had built the business around me, and everything of value still largely resided inside my mind. I didn't have the bandwidth to think about how to fix it, but I knew we had a problem.

After weeks of staring at my ringing phone and being physically unable to answer it, I couldn't take it any longer. I messaged my management team, told them I wouldn't make it in the next day and didn't know when I would be back.

I also told them what was happening to me.

They would have been concerned about how to manage the business without me, but they didn't show it. The message was: 'Andy, you just get yourself right. We'll take care of the business.'

I turned my phone off and went back to sleep. With that conversation out of the way, it was time to focus on my recovery.

Chapter 20

The Rebuild

The panic attacks and anxiety, combined with the ridiculous amount of running I was doing, meant that I had lost a lot of weight. I was struggling to swallow and digest any food, and I was only sleeping two to three hours per night. Some nights I wouldn't fall asleep until 5am. It's not a weight loss program I would recommend to anyone.

I knew this lifestyle wasn't sustainable, and eventually, after several months of a living hell, my high stress levels brought on ulcerative colitis. Essentially, ulcerative colitis is a hereditary illness caused by ulcers developing inside your colon, which start to bleed, making trips to the toilet very frequent and painful. It stops you from eating or drinking, your inflammation levels go through the roof and the stomach cramps are paralysing. My dad has suffered from UC for as long as I can remember, and at its worst, he can't spend twenty minutes in the car or away from a toilet. It's largely a psychological issue as well, and once you start to worry about it, you're done.

I vividly recall some of the worst days, where the smallest amount of stress would send me into a tailspin. I remember being hunched over the bed in the middle of the day, literally feeling the ulcers bursting inside my body and the blood trickling down into my colon. All I could do was curl up in the foetal position on the floor and wait for the pain to subside.

By this stage, I'd lost 20 kilograms, my skin started changing colour and I was in constant pain. I had never experienced ulcerative colitis so I ignored a lot of the obvious warning signs. But by this time I realised I was in a fair bit of trouble, and made the long-overdue decision to check myself into hospital.

The measurement of inflammation within the body is referred to as the C-reactive protein (CRP) level. Essentially it's measured in milligrams of inflammation per litre of blood. A standard reading in a healthy person is less than 5mg/L. A high CRP is more than 10mg/L, and anything at or above 100mg/L is a severe elevation that requires urgent care. My CRP was at 250mg/L, meaning I was suffering from sepsis and needed to be placed on a drip at short notice before things became dire. The look of concern on the doctor's face told me all I needed to know.

When I came out of hospital, my inflammation levels had started to stabilise, but I had a long road back to recovery. I was nowhere near fit enough to return to work, and even leaving the house was too much on the bad days. I was bedridden for twenty hours a day, unable to roll over without enduring crippling stomach pains. I spent that time listening to meditation, using that as my first building block to recovery.

On a positive note, all the work we had done to build a strong team was paying dividends. Once they realised how unwell I was, everyone sprang into action and took it upon themselves to take control of the business. Good decisions were being made every day that I had nothing to do with. I am forever grateful to the team for their support during my dark days; it was one less thing to worry about when my plate was full of challenges.

I chatted to my business coach, Leigh, about my struggles and found out that his wife, Liz, was a highly accomplished life coach. 'Life coach' is not a job title I would've given much respect to in my younger days, but when we caught up to discuss a plan to move forward with, it sounded like exactly what I needed. For the next three months, they worked in tandem; Leigh focused on optimising business performance (as he had for years), and Liz focused on optimising my own performance, which was a much more slow and painful process. We caught up twice a week for an hour, working on mental tools and coping mechanisms to help me rebuild myself on the inside and essentially rewire my mind. Liz suggested that I stop running when I suffered from these attacks, as she believed it helped to overcome the feeling at the time but in the longer term it was only winding me up even more. It was time for more mindfulness, meditation and deep breathing. I still went for runs, but only when I felt good about things, so it created a positive association.

Although I hadn't been drinking much, I cut out alcohol completely for a few months. And thanks to my new ulcerative colitis diagnosis, I was restricted to a very bland and boring diet of steamed vegetables and white meats without seasoning – nothing that would flare up my symptoms.

Life was dull but necessarily so, and I slowly embarked on the road to recovery.

After a month or so, I tried going back into the office. If I'd had a good sleep (which at this stage was four or five hours), I would message the team excitedly and tell them I was coming in. I still remember the feeling of anticipation as I drove to the office. But more often than not, I would be sitting in a meeting, my hands would start shaking and sweat would appear on my shirt. I would meekly excuse myself from the room and head back up the highway, throw my soaking clothes in the washing machine, lie back in bed and stare dejectedly at the ceiling.

Over the next few months, things started to improve. I got more sleep. I ate more regularly and put some weight back on. My complexion returned to something resembling a human being.

Looking back on that period, the whole episode lasted around a year, and the worst of it had a hold on me for six months, but it felt like an eternity. The tools for my recovery were fairly typical: a healthy diet; making sure I had plenty of sleep and the odd nap during the day; spending plenty of time in nature; and surrounding myself with friends and family. Shedding the traditional norms of a male friendship and being completely open about my feelings made a world of difference. This vulnerability also helped to unlock some of my friends' own innermost feelings, and I added many layers to some of my closest relationships throughout this time. Sometimes I would plan to catch up with a mate, only to fall at the final hurdle and let them know I wasn't feeling up to it, and their understanding helped to eliminate any of the guilt that can creep in at times.

I was able to confront my demons, put a plan into place and work my backside off to get myself back on track, meaning that it was a fairly rapid recovery. Having said that, I'm not dismissive in the slightest of those who suffer long-term depression and anxiety, and especially those who have faced significant trauma in their lives.

Once I felt like I was back to 90 per cent of full health, I sat down and wrote some notes about my experience. Sometimes I preferred to go for a walk and record a voice memo. I also made some voice recordings during my darkest moments, rambling incoherently about whatever came into my head at the time. I listened back to them when I was feeling good, wanting to understand who I was at that moment in time. It's quite triggering to listen to them now, but they are a powerful motivator to never let myself go back to that place.

I made a commitment that I would share my story. I have since recorded a handful of podcasts on the topic, presented at a conference on my mental health battles and mentored a number of entrepreneurs and start-ups. My message is clear: if you are driven and passionate, you don't have to suffer the consequences like I did. You just need to identify the early warning signs and take time to look after yourself along the way.

I'd like to think that my story has had a positive impact on the industry. I remember one presentation I made to a few hundred of my peers at the Smart Energy Conference, where I opened up about how bad things had become. I didn't have a script in mind, I just spoke from the heart. I shed a few tears throughout the presentation and had to stop and compose myself a few times. After I finished, the conversations I had were incredibly powerful. People lined up to thank me, and someone I'd never met gave me a big hug. One guy came up and introduced me to his dad, a stubborn old bloke who runs an electrical business from his garage in a country town, and refuses to take a day off. He said to his dad, 'See what this bloke has been through? Mum and I keep telling you that if you don't slow down, you're going to kill yourself.' We spoke about his situation for a while and I feel like he came away with a new perspective on life.

I think society in general, and men in particular, have come a long way in opening up about our struggles. I was raised in a very blokey and macho environment, with these conversations rarely happening within the walls of the footy club. Every conversation like this breaks down the stigma and I hope that my honesty will encourage someone else to open up to their mates if they are doing it tough.

After this ordeal, the other commitment I made was to Kel. We needed to ensure that the business didn't rely on me as heavily. My health battles had become a blessing in disguise, forcing us to think about how to make Gippsland Solar more sustainable. As Kel pointed out: 'There's no point in being the richest person in the graveyard.'

Up until this point, I hadn't given a moment's thought to a succession plan and I had certainly not considered an acquisition. I had thought that one day the kids might take it over, and we had jokingly watched our three boys negotiating a trade for footy cards and appointed the future CEO based on their performance.

Kel and I had started this business and set the direction, but it now ran off its own energy. With our annual revenue in the tens of millions at that stage, and with the size of the market opportunity growing rapidly, it was quickly becoming much bigger than we had ever planned for. Holding it back was not feasible. It felt like the business wanted to grow regardless of our own needs and desires, and our team wanted it to grow too. As Leigh said, 'You've got a tiger by the tail.'

We conducted a review of how robust our systems and processes were. The unsurprising answer was 'not very'. We had built an enviable reputation and created a business with entrepreneurial flair, one that was able to stay nimble and pivot through the peaks and troughs of the solar coaster. But we hadn't invested in our procedures, and our internal governance was sorely lacking. We didn't even conduct regular stocktakes or require anyone to sign a document when they took products from the warehouse (which likely explained the frequent and unexplained gaps in our stock levels during the early days).

Essentially, we had enjoyed all the 'fun' parts of growing a business, but we hadn't done the work.

Not only did we need to build the hard elements to strengthen the business, but we also needed to focus on the soft side. I still got dozens of calls every week from my team, wanting to run something by me before they made a judgement call. Many of these issues were relatively insignificant, but I had created a culture where everything was run by me, and that culture permeated through the workforce. So I started asking them how *they* thought we should handle the situation and probing them as to why. Most of the time their judgement was spot-on, so we would make the call together. But I would remind them that they knew the right thing to do, and from now on, they were to feel empowered to make that call without me.

If their judgement call was wrong, we didn't get too hung up on it. I've made plenty of these bad calls over the years myself. It's important to have the freedom to fail, and to learn the lessons as you go.

It did take some major adjustment on my behalf. The feeling of becoming less relevant took me a while to become accustomed to, and I would find myself poking around and interfering with things when I felt left out. But I tried to remind myself that this was the goal.

Everyone wants to feel empowered in their role. Learning how to 'lead from behind' is an acquired skill, but one that is critical if you want to develop your leaders in their own right. This attitude will quickly cascade through your organisation and make everyone feel that they are valued. As a result, they will invariably take more responsibility and treat the business like their own.

For the first time, I was able to take more regular breaks and commit more time and energy to my family. It was a lesson learned the hard way, but one that greatly improved my performance as a leader and made me a much better person to be around at home.

Chapter 21

Knocks on the Door

As we developed these systems and processes, coincidentally, large corporations started approaching us. With so much at stake in the industry, big companies were swallowing up small solar companies every other week, desperate to fast-track their capability and leverage the incredible opportunities within the energy transition.

The first approach we received was from one of the biggest players in the energy retail space: a multi-billion-dollar juggernaut for whom the cost of purchasing of Gippsland Solar would be comparable to ashtray change. But we weren't encouraged by the revolving door of relationship managers who came down the highway, started a conversation and then left the company. The whole experience gave an impression that they were totally devoid of culture, and the idea of sitting in middle management of an organisation like that (and selling that dream to my team) left me feeling very uncomfortable.

The other approach was from a private equity firm, which had very deep pockets. They wanted to purchase a select few solar businesses along the eastern seaboard, aggregate them and turn the group into the largest solar procurement company in Australia. It was interesting at first, but when we heard the way they spoke about our business and the opportunity to 'fatten up the P&L' so we could all make a lot of money, we felt that our people would soon become expendable, and we had no interest in seeing Gippsland Solar go that way.

I decided to entertain these approaches and go through the process, mostly as a way of gaining some free professional development. By learning what companies at the big end of town were looking for, we could make better decisions in how we structured our business for the future. I'm sure they were also using the process to learn the secret to our success.

Around this time, we started to win some significant commercial contracts in New South Wales and Queensland. One of these opportunities was an installation for the largest private shopping centre in Australia. It would be the biggest solar and storage project of its kind in the country, with 2600kW of solar and a whopping 10,000kWh battery. This is the equivalent of 740 Tesla Powerwalls! It was the kind of project that would change the game and put Gippsland Solar up in lights within all the major industry publications. The only issue was that we had neither the personnel nor the balance sheet to handle the outlay for these projects. We maintained our commitment not to take on debt to grow the business, adding financial pressure to the melting pot of issues that were already swirling around inside my head in the middle of the night.

The pressure was building again.

In mid-2019, I headed over to Munich for the Intersolar Conference with two of my team. While we were there, I met two guys who worked at RACV. At first, I didn't understand why two senior managers from RACV would travel across the globe for an energy conference.

For those who aren't familiar with them, RACV stands for the Royal Automobile Club of Victoria. It was established in 1903 as a motoring organisation. Since then, it has grown to become one of the largest member organisations in Victoria, if not the country. The RACV group (including all entities) employs thousands of people, turns over several billion dollars and has over two million members. As a member-owned mutual organisation, RACV has accumulated dozens of business interests, which span car, home and boat insurance, roadside assist, an incredible array of holiday resorts across the country, home trades/services and more. In terms of its history, financial capability, and depth and breadth of its network, there are few organisations like RACV.

It was many things, but an energy company it was not.

But upon doing some research, it appeared that the strategy was shifting within RACV. They had already started a division called RACV Solar, which had a team of five employees, and they were installing a system or two every week. It was interesting, but my mind was fully occupied by daily business and personal challenges, so I didn't think much more about it.

When I returned to Australia, the RACV team reached out again to follow up. They were running a tender for a partner to deliver their residential solar installations, and we were asked to put ourselves forward. Given the size of their ambition, it was a big deal. We were already stretched very thin and I was concerned that taking on such a high-profile contract and performing poorly would place our reputation at risk. I sent them an email to politely decline, indicating that we weren't confident that we could deliver the contract to the level that RACV was worthy of. They selected one of our largest competitors to deliver the rollout.

It was probably the first time I had walked away from a big opportunity because I didn't feel we had the capacity to handle it, and I was kicking myself about the decision for weeks.

Several months later, I was out quoting a few jobs in Gippsland in my electric vehicle and realised that I had left myself short of range to make it home. I had to pop into the RACV resort at Inverloch to charge the car for fifteen minutes. It was only the second time I had used the charger there in four years.

While I was sitting in the car, I looked up and saw two guys in fluoro shirts standing on the roof. For anyone who has run a solar business, you'll know that the sight of mysterious hi-vis people on roofs activates all your senses. I wondered if they might be solar installers quoting a job for the RACV resorts, but figured it was likely just a couple of air-con installers fixing some plant equipment.

But I couldn't shake the nagging curiosity so I went to investigate. Sure enough, one of our competitors' vans was in the car park!

I happened to know a guy who had started working at RACV in the solar team, so I rang him and asked if they were installing solar on their resorts. He said that he wasn't aware of any plans, but he would make a few calls internally to confirm.

He rang me back half an hour later and said they *were* installing solar. In fact, they were planning to roll out nearly 3MW of solar projects (about 10,000 solar panels) across all their resorts in Victoria, Queensland and Tasmania. Still stewing on our decision to decline the last RACV tender, I was burning for the opportunity to win this one.

The procurement process was already well underway, but this time they were only selecting national companies. After convincing them that we also had national capability, I wrangled Gippsland Solar onto the shortlist. We had to get every site inspection, modelling and proposal done in seven days, covering thousands of kilometres. Like many times before, we would bite off way more than we could chew and then start chewing like crazy.

After progressing through the stages, we were shortlisted against one of our largest and most formidable competitors – one that we enjoyed beating (and hated losing to) the most. The stakes were high.

That Friday afternoon at 4.55pm, the phone rang.

'Is this a good news call or a bad news call?'

'It's good news, Andy. Strap yourself in, we're going ahead with you.' I dropped the phone out of pure exhilaration.

Now we had to deliver.

We directed a huge number of resources into the RACV contract and onboarded three of the best contracting teams we knew. It wasn't just the size of the projects, it was the complexity. They were huge resorts with no obvious way to run cabling, and we had to find a way to deliver these projects without turning the power off and without impacting on the hundreds of members who were staying there at the time. Sometimes we only had a two-hour window where we could make any noise, which is not easy when you're installing systems on the roof!

With hundreds of residential jobs in our pipeline, and a handful of other significant projects to juggle at the same time, everyone was feeling the pressure. We were like the proverbial duck, calm on the surface but paddling like crazy underneath. I could sense the team was feeling depleted and I didn't have enough energy in reserve to energise them. I started to go backwards in my recovery and those familiar feelings started to wash over me.

One day, I received a call from RACV's Head of Energy, who asked me to come in for a meeting. He told me that Neil Taylor, the CEO, would be in attendance. My blood ran cold.

'Uh, sure thing. Is everything going well with the installs?'

His tone lifted. 'Oh yep, everything is great. We just want to have a chat with you.'

Despite his reassurance, I didn't sleep much for the next few nights and shuffled into that meeting feeling exhausted. I was also full of trepidation (and fear) about why I was being summoned to a meeting with the CEO with no context.

I was greeted by a room full of heavy hitters from RACV, but tried to play it cool. After a meandering ten-minute conversation with Neil that covered everything from football to Shakespeare and the shoes I was wearing, he cut to the chase.

'We're serious about getting into solar. We've built a great little internal team here, but I want to speed things up. We want to know if you'd be interested in selling your business to RACV.'

I vividly recall my feeling at that moment. After being under so much pressure for the past few years, I didn't feel like I could handle any more. I had been fighting battles every day, either internal or external, and had pushed myself to breaking point. I couldn't be the leader I needed to be, nor the husband or father that my family deserved. I felt like I had been bobbing in the ocean with waves crashing over me for a long time, and someone had just arrived and handed me a life raft.

I took a few breaths and composed myself. 'Uh sure, I'd be interested.'

Chapter 22

Exit Strategy

I could barely contain my excitement when I called Kel, who agreed that this was an opportunity we couldn't pass up.

Neither of us were overly keen on the previous approaches we had received, but this was different. A member-owned mutual organisation was a very different proposition to a private equity fund or a large corporate with shareholders. After we did some research on the values, employee engagement and lofty mission statement of RACV (to 'improve the lives of all Victorians'), it was clear that this was a once-in-a-lifetime opportunity. They were perhaps the only organisation that could afford to acquire us, yet were also seemingly aligned with our values.

But we also agreed that we wouldn't be comfortable about any deal that involved a minority stake or partial acquisition. The nature of founders and entrepreneurs is that we have plenty of vision and passion, but we aren't used to being told what to do. And if you are not aligned in some way, it can become ugly very quickly when both parties have skin in the game. For these reasons, Kel and I only felt comfortable selling 100 per cent of the business.

I also knew that if we resisted RACV's approach, they would acquire someone else. And not only would we likely lose the rest of the RACV resort contract, but it would also make one of our largest competitors very formidable indeed.

I took perhaps the biggest risk of my career.

When we came back together, I told RACV that I wanted this deal to happen as much as they did, and I was convinced that they were the right partner for Gippsland Solar and its people. But after careful consideration, I wasn't prepared to accept a partial acquisition.

I gave them two options. They could acquire 0 per cent of Gippsland Solar or 100 per cent of Gippsland Solar.

I don't think they were expecting that response, and the rest of the meeting was subdued. We shook hands, and Neil said they would be in touch.

I couldn't focus on anything else. It was the hardest few weeks of my working life, trying to lead the business with my head completely out of the game. It was gut-wrenching.

Neil called me in for another meeting.

They were in.

I can't recall anything that happened in the meeting after that – it's all a blur. All the years of grind and setbacks were about to culminate in the deal of a lifetime. If everything went smoothly and the sale went through, it would be one of the biggest acquisitions that had ever happened in the industry.

Once the euphoria of the meeting with RACV wore off, I realised that we would have no shortage of challenges to manage. The due diligence period was expected to run for six months. And, as with everything that RACV did, it was going to be very thorough and presumably expensive, consuming a lot of our collective headspace. I would need to manage my own energy very carefully.

I couldn't speak to my staff about the proposed acquisition and I was aware that any leaks could impact the deal. This was extremely hard to come to terms with, as I had always prided myself on being open and transparent with my team. Suddenly, I became secretive and evasive. Without being privy to what was happening, my team was wondering why I was so withdrawn. Most of them assumed I was back in the deep hole that I had found myself last year.

One day, my Gippsland team were sitting in the Traralgon office, and an army of well-dressed men and women from the RACV due diligence team and legal firm turned up. They smiled and said their good mornings, then walked straight into the conference room with me and closed the door. Unsurprisingly, the place was abuzz.

'Are we being audited?'

'Investigated by WorkSafe?'

'Have we just won a massive contract?'

They didn't know what was happening, good or bad, but they knew it was big.

When we won the RACV tender, one of the largest rollouts

in Australia, it was significant news across the industry. When it also tied in with RACV's announcement that they were investing heavily into their solar and energy division, it set tongues wagging across the industry. When I kept my head down and remained uncharacteristically quiet about the RACV partnership, everyone knew something big was brewing and drew their own conclusions.

The natural industry response to the swirling rumours of our acquisition was to pull out all the stops to kill the deal.

Tall poppy syndrome is a huge problem in Australia, and I felt the full effect of it. 'Customers' (who we had no record of in the system) would contact RACV to say they had a horrible experience with us. They would call my character into question, implying that I had a dubious reputation. Someone (presumably one of our competitors) even drove past our installation at a RACV resort, took a photo from an awkward angle so it looked like we were standing right at the edge of the roof, and emailed it directly to Neil Taylor. We had to give RACV a tour of the roof in question and show them that with the way our fall protection was set up, it was physically impossible for us to be within 3 metres of a live edge.

RACV's commercial team were firm but fair. You know you've ended in the right position when both parties feel like they've given away a little bit of value. And you must always remember that once the negotiations are complete, you all need to move in together. Maintaining a warm relationship throughout the discussions is key.

We found the best lawyer we could afford, a small but wonderful firm in East Melbourne, and it was almost humorous when we met

with the RACV legal team. On one side of the table, there was me
and my lawyer, Simon, with a notepad and pen. On the other side,
there was an army of the most reputable (and presumably expensive)
lawyers in the industry, with support staff to set up their IT and
systems before each meeting. Much like the Camberwell Grammar
tender, it felt like a scene from *The Castle*, where I had engaged Dennis
Denuto to stare down the High Court. However, it quickly became
apparent that Simon was an absolute weapon in this environment,
and his depth of knowledge, warmth and humility was the perfect
fit for me. He was also firm but fair, and everyone at RACV enjoyed
dealing with him.

I largely confined myself to a non-speaking role throughout these
meetings, partly because I didn't want to embarrass myself, and partly
because I was soaking up the language and conduct of these forums.
At one point they were debating a specific detail on our warranty
document, something that would have had almost zero impact on
their liability. It was going around and around in circles for maybe
twenty minutes between the lawyers, so I chimed in: 'I'm sitting here
trying to calculate the hourly rate of the people in this room. I think
we can all agree to move on and stop running the bill up for RACV.'

They looked at each other, smiled wryly and moved on.

As we signed a term sheet and edged closer to formalising the deal,
I was relieved to be able to give my team a clearer understanding of
what had been going on throughout the year. I told them I didn't
know what was going to happen, but either way it would be a great
thing for Gippsland Solar and for them. Either we ended up being

acquired by RACV and becoming one of the largest and most stable companies in the industry, or we would gain invaluable improvements to our systems and processes, ensuring that we would charge ahead with a renewed sense of self-confidence. I wasn't sure I believed that, as I knew it would be a tremendous let-down if the deal didn't go ahead, but I had to portray a sense of strength to calm their anxiety.

The last couple of months were the hardest, as an increasing number of people knew that an announcement was imminent. Our competitors seized on this uncertainty, either using it against us in the market or trying to destabilise us from within. I tried to stay calm and composed, fully aware that people were studying my body language, and that my energy (positive or negative) was rubbing off on them. Externally, I stopped doing all media, choosing to put my entire focus into supporting my team and staying on message. Internally, I told my team that I had always made business decisions to provide the best opportunities for them, and they had to take me at my word that I would never do anything to compromise those values.

RACV had set a completion date of 14 December 2019. The lead-up to Christmas was always a crazy time with project deadlines, stock shortages, unreasonable customer expectations and the side effects of a tiring year impacting our team as we crawled towards the finish line. It was a flurry of activity in November and early December, tying up loose ends and responding to final due diligence requests, and I was back to sleeping only a few hours a night. We were also keeping an eye on a virus that was believed to have spread from China in the last few weeks. It was a turbulent time in every conceivable way.

We set up a meeting room in our Mirboo North office on the 14th of December, with my lawyer, accountant and some of the senior management team huddled around a table. Emails were flying back and forth between our team and the RACV lawyers, while I sat with my back to the wall, logged into my Bendigo Bank account, hitting refresh every ten seconds. With a last-minute hiccup in the process, along with a series of concerning emails from my health and safety manager about the spread of what they were calling 'novel coronavirus', I hit refresh for the last time at 12.20pm, saw the account balance and slammed my computer screen shut.

It all hit me at once.

I was overcome with joy and relief, my body shaking uncontrollably and tears flowing freely. After all the years of struggle and sacrifice, and putting everything we had back into the business, we had pulled it off. There were plenty of challenges on the road ahead, but I would never have to worry about our financial freedom again.

That night, we bought the fancy clothes pegs.

Chapter 23

Transitions

The week following the acquisition was like nothing I've ever experienced.

This was one of the largest and most respected organisations and brands in Australia acquiring one of the best-known solar businesses in the country. I did a double-take when I opened the *Financial Review* and saw the news of our acquisition featuring prominently. I pinched myself at how we had started in the garage with a $6 ad and an invoice book in Mirboo North and somehow ended up at this point ten years later.

We completed over twenty interviews that day, as I was shepherded around from one recording studio to another. In hindsight, I would love to have been more present for my team and to savour this moment with them, but the first few days were largely mapped out for me.

I had agreed to the acquisition for a number of reasons. Of course, the money was important, and it was satisfying to secure my financial future and provide for the family. But as I matured over the years, I was less obsessed with the idea of making money, and now only saw it as a by-product of running a great business and doing the right thing by people. There must be something else that drives you, otherwise you just end up in the empty and pointless pursuit of trying to make more money.

The opportunity to make a big impact on the industry was also a key factor in my decision. Almost overnight, I had been thrust into one of the most influential and sought-after roles in the industry, and I could scarcely believe my luck.

When news of the acquisition broke, a number of people questioned why RACV was making this investment. Why would a motoring organisation acquire a solar panel business? I thought the strategy was spot-on, especially as RACV was getting in at the early stages of the electric vehicle revolution. Consumers were looking for a company they could trust to guide them on the journey to an all-electric home, with all elements of their life (including their cars) powered by renewable energy. Few organisations have implicit trust like RACV does, and the power of its balance sheet was also a huge advantage.

Our strategy clearly made sense to the market as well. Not long after our deal was announced, RACQ (the Queensland version of RACV) followed suit, acquiring a majority stake in a solar company in Queensland called GEM Energy. Then, a short time after that,

RAA in South Australia acquired a solar company called Living Energy. These were both very astute business moves, with Jack Hooper (CEO of GEM Energy) and brothers Ben and David Lovell (founders of Living Energy) having established a terrific reputation throughout the industry.

After the cameras and scripts had been packed up and the fanfare died down, my elation turned to uncertainty and doubt. I had never worked in the corporate environment before, and frankly had never wanted to. But RACV had placed a great deal of faith in us, and now we had to deliver.

As part of the acquisition, we also established the RACV Solar board. It comprised the chair, Nicole, a highly experienced professional who had spent decades in the corporate world, who was the EGM of Home and Energy for RACV, and to whom I indirectly reported now. We also had Michael, the CFO of RACV, an intellectual giant who had been the CFO for a listed company before this role.

And then there was me.

I had never sat on a board and hadn't even completed my company director's course. I had zero business qualifications. I hadn't even finished Year 10! The learning curve was steep, to say the least, and RACV quickly sent me off to complete the course at the Australian Institute for Company Directors, recognising that it was well overdue for the CEO of a company of our size. I confess to not understanding many of the acronyms that were thrust in my direction at first, but I threw myself into it wholeheartedly and had enough humility to acknowledge what I didn't know. With so many heavy hitters in the room, I also used it as a tremendous networking opportunity, of course!

I was worried about how this change would impact our team. I kept reinforcing that while there would be some structural changes, our 'GipSol' culture would remain intact. But I knew there would be things that were beyond my control. I was instructed to move our team into Bourke Street, alongside RACV's other subsidiary businesses.

The RACV head office in Bourke Street is breathtaking on first impression, especially when you've come from a working environment with makeshift offices and second-hand chairs. Taking up almost an entire city block and soaring into the sky, the RACV HQ and City Club features over thirty floors of offices and accommodation, an underground dining room and wine cellar, restaurants, a library, a world-class billiards room (where they host the Australian Snooker Championships), conference rooms, a massive remote working space with a cafe, and a rooftop function centre with an incredible open-roof viewing platform. There's also a huge underground gym and car park with EV charging, which was the icing on the cake.

But my team were less than impressed about having to move. Prior to the acquisition, we had opened a sales office in a funky laneway in Richmond, and my team loved it; it was a relaxed place full of music and laughter where everyone could be themselves. The move into RACV's office made good business sense, but it wasn't a popular decision within our team.

If there's one thing I've learned early on, it is the importance of being aligned. Leah Mether, a friend and colleague of mine, nailed it in her book *Steer Through the Storm*. Her message is: 'Debate in private. Unite in public.' It's important to advocate heavily for your team and push back with conviction if you feel passionate about something. But once the decision has been made, you need to move on quickly and present a united front. Any sense of 'us vs them' between myself and RACV would have quickly become destabilising and impacted heavily on our culture. I didn't always get it right, but I tried my hardest.

This is not the time nor place to drag out the dirty laundry, but you can appreciate there were plenty of times when a deep breath was required (on both sides!). There was no shortage of jostling for position and trying to establish the rules of engagement, which I had fully expected but still struggled with at times.

I would have been quite painful for RACV to deal with as well. I had agreed to sell our business but didn't want to relinquish any form of control. In hindsight, I was protective of my team to a fault, and at times I felt like a shepherd protecting his flock. But although my team saw me as the CEO and the top of the food chain, the reality now was that I was merely a middle manager in a very large organisation. Sometimes I felt like I was in a vice, with a combination of the top-down and bottom-up pressure becoming too much to handle.

But for all the challenges we had to navigate, my god it was exciting. For ten years we had been the little engine that could, huffing and puffing and achieving things far beyond our perceived capability.

We were cashflow-constrained, devoid of many critical systems and processes, and most of our success came from pure determination and buy-in from the team. Now we had a vast business network to tap into, and found ourselves freed up from the cashflow challenges that can stifle the ambitions of many small and medium-sized businesses. As one of my competitors said when he rang to congratulate me, 'I've always said that RACV was the sleeping giant of the solar industry, and I have a feeling you're about to wake them up.'

As you can probably imagine, there were times when I butted heads with RACV on our approach, especially around marketing and communications. Again, it was about picking and choosing my battles. Sometimes you need to challenge an existing approach, and sometimes you need to respect the history and traditions of the organisation. I'd like to think that the result of this natural tension was a positive for RACV. I'm sure there were a few eyerolls over the years when I went off-piste, and a reluctant acceptance of 'That's just Andy!'

Once we developed a nice working rhythm, there were some tremendous wins. We took up a highly successful major sponsorship of the Melbourne Renegades WBBL team, which aligned with our commitment to bring more women into renewable energy. We also signed up Gary Ablett Jr, AFL legend and Hall of Fame inductee, as our brand ambassador, and installed solar and a battery on his house (and for his mum, Sue, who lived next door). Gary was a terrific guy to deal with, and I found him to be extremely humble and generous with his time. The partnership with Gary gave us a significant boost as we expanded into the Geelong and south-west region.

But of all the positives that RACV brought to our business, it was the power of a trusted brand that trumped everything. This level of trust is important in so many industries, but particularly in a turbulent sector like solar and battery storage. Nationally there are over 1 million systems installed by companies that are no longer in business, with over 1000 companies having gone into receivership or administration since 2010. And with the performance warranty on a solar panel lasting for twenty-five or thirty years, it's understandable that people don't know where to turn.

There were many areas where we had to align with RACV. I completely understood the need for uniformity in areas such as safety, policies and procedures, governance and risk frameworks, and business planning. But I was also conscious to keep an element of separation between our business and the mothership. I was incredibly proud of the culture we had built at Gippsland Solar, and felt that it was key to our success. By identifying our own mission statement, core values and ways of collaborating with each other, we could achieve the right balance of RACV influence without disrupting what has been a tremendously successful business model. Our employee engagement scores remained at satisfyingly high levels for the next few years, so I'd say we struck the right balance.

In an uncertain business environment, the support of RACV was a key reason I agreed to the acquisition. And with the unprecedented period we were about to head into, I was going to need all the support I could muster.

Chapter 24

Under Fire

The Black Summer bushfires broke out of the forests on 30 December 2019, only two weeks after the acquisition. They devastated our region, killing thirty-three people and millions of animals, and burning through 10 million hectares across Gippsland, up in the north-east of the state, and into southern New South Wales. It was a horrific experience for everyone involved, and several years on, the scars still remain.

We had headed down to our onsite caravan at Waratah Bay, near Wilsons Promontory in South Gippsland. It was our 'happy place', a tranquil little township surrounded by the Cape Liptrap National Park, straddling a picture-perfect beach filled with rockpools, waterfalls and amazing surf breaks. It was a place where we had escaped the rat race and soothed our battered souls for many years, and one that also played a key role in my recovery. After the biggest year we ever had, full of stress and uncertainty, that summer was meant to be the happiest few weeks of our lives.

After a scorching 40-degree day spent swimming and flapping around in the waves, we were enjoying a glass of champagne with friends, toasting the sale of the business, when the smoke appeared on the horizon.

The whole region became blanketed in thick smoke, and some areas were almost pitch-black in the middle of the day. After a flurry of phone calls and messages, I found out that many of our team were in the path of the fires, evacuated from their homes or desperately fighting to protect their communities. The radio station in Mallacoota had gone offline after the electricity grid went down, and people were fleeing on boats. It was terrifying.

Neil Taylor rang me on New Year's Eve and asked how everyone was doing. I told him that we were all fine for now, but obviously very worried about how the next few days would play out.

'I told you RACV would support you, and I am good for that,' he said. 'Let me know if there's anything I or my team can do to help in Gippsland.'

Neil was true to his word. Within forty-eight hours, and with the full weight of RACV behind us, we had mobilised a huge support package for the impacted region. We arranged for their Nationwide Towing business to send tow trucks up to East Gippsland with hay, tools and fencing equipment to assist the immediate rebuild. We organised fifty generators to be stored at our Bairnsdale warehouse and provided them free of charge to locals who had no electricity.

We also made a significant donation to the Gippsland Emergency Relief Fund.

Once the fires subsided, we took stock of the damage across the region. The electricity grid was decimated throughout East Gippsland, with poles and transmission lines badly damaged, leaving around 130,000 people without power. I spoke to my contacts at AusNet, and they were concerned that it would take weeks or months to restore power to the most impacted and remote regions.

Now the real work would begin, and renewable energy was to play a key role in the rebuild.

We put a call out on social media to see how we could provide support and were flooded with cries for help from communities who needed emergency electricity. Some of our engineers and electricians were more than happy to cut their holidays short to assist. Our suppliers of solar panels stepped up to donate some product, and Tesla provided emergency battery packs with only a few hours' notice. Within a few days, we had designed and constructed a handful of standalone solar and battery systems, designed on pallets and frames with concrete pads so they could be trucked in to provide emergency electricity supply for the most affected towns. Those systems were supplied free of charge and used to power wildlife shelters to care for injured wildlife, and community halls to provide refrigeration and fresh drinking water for communities. We also contacted the radio station in Mallacoota and donated a large battery system with a backup generator, so they could continue to broadcast for several days if an emergency like this occurred in the future. Hopefully, it will never be needed.

The bushfire recovery also gave birth to RACV's Solar in the Regions initiative. We committed $1 million to providing free solar and battery systems to twenty-eight towns across rural Victoria, which would provide reliable electricity and peace of mind in the event of future emergencies. We started in the towns that were the most impacted by the bushfires, replacing their makeshift systems with permanent and reliable sources of electricity. We then expanded it to those towns that were increasingly at risk of these disasters in the future, creating a 'place of last resort' where the community could gather and be safe together.

It was an incredible amount of work by the whole team, but it had a monumental impact. It was heartwarming and highly emotional travelling around to these communities throughout the program, sharing laughs and tears with them, and hearing their stories of resilience and community spirit. Several years later, I'm still getting a spine chill as I reflect on it.

The horror of Black Summer, and the recovery work afterwards, was a galvanising time for the business. When news of the sale was made public and we announced that we would rebrand as RACV Solar, there were plenty of comments in the street and on social media about how we had 'sold out'. I had been given a firm commitment that we would retain our Latrobe Valley team and HQ, but there was understandable scepticism. I was abused in a cafe one day as I ate my lunch and received some scathing private messages about how we were turning our backs on Gippsland. Our commitment and the incredible efforts of our team during the rebuild showed that we were still there to support the local region, but at a scale that Gippsland Solar could never have imagined.

The Black Summer ordeal was also a pivotal moment for the transition to renewable energy. The devastating impact the fires had on the electricity grid shone a light on how vulnerable we were to natural disasters, and to grid failures in general. Some of the affected towns only had a handful of homes and used very little electricity, but they required dozens of kilometres of poles and wires (through densely packed bushland) to supply them. The township of Mallacoota has suffered regular and prolonged outages for as long as I can remember. Unfortunately, regulations required these remote towns to be connected to the grid, even though it made no technical or financial sense. We worked with AusNet and the State Government on some initiatives to make these remote communities more energy-resilient, which resulted in several programs to deliver community microgrids and shore up their electricity supply. Hopefully a change in policy will be next, allowing the most remote regions to source their electricity from renewable sources.

With each of these significant events in Gippsland (the mine fire, closure of Hazelwood and Black Summer), the region has taken significant strides towards the renewable energy transition.

While the Black Summer bushfires decimated our region, the aftermath and recovery followed a familiar path. Unfortunately we have become accustomed to these awful events over the last few decades, and the short-, medium- and long-term stages of the rebuild are fairly predictable. But there was another devastating event headed our way that would throw the entire world into a state of chaos, and have an even bigger impact on our business.

Around this time, the virus that had been somewhat on our radar was looking to be a serious threat. The first few cases of Covid-19 started appearing on our shores, and there were rumblings in the media about closing airports, and even lockdowns within the community to halt the spread of the virus.

The rest, as they say, is history. Covid would go on to devastate all parts of the Australian societal and business landscape. There would be thousands of deaths and thousands of businesses closing their doors in the years ahead. We would be forced to temporarily shut down our business a number of times, for months in total. Residential installations were banned, punching a massive hole in our business performance.

Most of the time in business, success comes down to hard work and perseverance. But occasionally it's pure luck. I still struggle to comprehend how fortunate we were on our business journey. We began Gippsland Solar right at the very start of the 'boom time', when residential and commercial installations were about to grow exponentially, and with little competition in the Latrobe Valley. We rode the wave for ten years, completing our exit only a few weeks before the pandemic would have a devastating impact on businesses across the country. I'm sure if the negotiations had dragged out a few more weeks and into the new year, the deal would have been off the table (or at least under review), and we would have faced the most challenging business environment of our generation all by ourselves.

It worked out incredibly well for our team too. We would have had to let go of many exceptional people as lockdowns shook the solar industry to its foundations. The message from the RACV Solar board was: 'You just support your people and keep the team together. Once we weather the storm with our workforce intact, we will be able to rebound quickly.'

Despite lockdowns meaning we had to regularly cancel our installations, demand for solar and battery storage was at an all-time high. With the power of the RACV brand behind us, we enjoyed a rapid period of sales growth within our first twelve months. We were breaking records for the largest projects of their kind in Australia, having established ourselves as the provider of choice for governments, councils, building developers and blue-chip brands. With a combination of record sales figures and being hampered by restrictions, we had a staggering pipeline of work to deliver. We didn't publicise the volumes that we were installing, but we had become one of the largest handful of companies in the country, and clearly the largest in Victoria in the premium price bracket. A nice flow-on effect from establishing this reputation was that we attracted the very best people in the industry and built a formidable team. It was very satisfying to reflect on how far we had come from the early days of Gippsland Solar when I had to beg people to come and work for us.

With this frantic period behind us, it was now time for the next stage of the journey: to find the next Gippsland Solar out there and make their dreams come true too.

Chapter 25

When the Tables Are Turned

With our newly minted business plan in hand at the end of 2020, we got to work. Our strategy was all about growth, and I was tasked with identifying any opportunities to take RACV Solar forward.

We looked at dozens of solar companies for potential acquisition during my time at the helm. Once it was well known around industry circles that RACV was looking to expand through acquisition, my inbox was full of business owners hoping to complete their own exit strategy. Some of the businesses we looked at were terrific operations and run by great leaders, but weren't the right size, timing or geographic fit to complement our strategy. Others were just plain bad news – 'fly-by-night' companies that had sprung up overnight and taken advantage of government rebates, leaving a trail of liability out there that they hoped someone else would pick up the tab for. They looked successful on paper and might pass a due diligence process, but a few calls around the industry told you everything you needed to know.

Despite meeting some quality companies within the Melbourne metro market, I found that regional businesses were a better fit for us. I love the values that country businesses are known for, largely because you can't be anonymous. As I've said to many people over the years, you could trust me because I live in a town of 2000 people. If I did the wrong thing by you, you'd see me coaching your son or daughter at weekend sport, or down at the IGA supermarket, at the school gate in the morning or at a committee meeting that night. No matter how big our business became, everyone knew where I lived, and people could (and did!) turn up at my front door to hold me accountable if I didn't return their calls.

Many of these smaller regional businesses were younger versions of Gippsland Solar. They were commonly husband-and-wife operations, where their employees were also their friends, and the business had their personal brand all over it. They did many things well but would benefit greatly from the structure and support that RACV could provide.

The first business we acquired was Great Ocean Solar and Electrical in Geelong, run by a young couple, Reece and Nikki. Like Gippsland Solar, it was a small business with big dreams, and everything they did was to an incredibly high standard. They worked hard and played hard, with the business operating hours often determined by the surf report that morning! You can always tell what the team will be like by meeting the owners, and it was clear that Reece and Nikki had assembled a fine collection of human beings in their workforce.

We started the conversation over a beer at the Ocean Grove Surf Lifesaving Club, where I spent a couple of hours just getting to know them as people, and what stage they were at in their professional and personal journey. With minimal work–life balance, a newborn child and a semi-renovated home in dire need of some attention, it was clear that this was a great opportunity for Reece and Nikki to take some pressure off themselves. It was equally clear that they would be a tremendous asset to RACV Solar, and their local reputation would ensure the success of this partnership.

I was very hands-on in the discussion with Reece and Nikki, having been in the exact same position myself a year earlier. I understood exactly how they would be feeling, and so I was able to walk them through the journey and provide comfort that they would be looked after.

After we acquired their business and invested in a new showroom and warehouse, several employees from competing businesses heard the news and wanted to jump on board. We managed to double the size of that business in a very short timeframe and carve out a significant market share in a very competitive region. We successfully delivered the largest community solar program in the region's history and became the go-to company for many of the local councils.

We enjoyed great success in most areas of Victoria, but the Bendigo region was still a black hole for us. No matter what we tried, we just couldn't gain a foothold in the market. The clearly dominant provider in Bendigo was a family-run business called Cola Solar.

I remembered them from a TV jingle, a terribly annoying but highly effective campaign that stayed in your head long after you turned the telly off.

We had crossed paths with Cola Solar in the market before. When we won the contract to install a 200kW system on the new Bendigo Hospital, which at the time was probably the largest solar installation in the Bendigo CBD, we were staying at a holiday park up the road for eight weeks, with our branded Gippsland Solar vehicles in the car park. Every few nights, the Cola Solar guys would cruise past our cabin at a very slow pace, peering out of their windows to let us know we were in their territory. After a few of these trips, some (presumably sarcastic) smiles and waves were exchanged between our teams.

I reached out to a mutual colleague and asked if there was a succession plan for Cola Solar, as I knew that the founders, Tony and Kaye, were in their mid-sixties. Within a few days, word filtered through the grapevine and Tony reached out. Once we completed the pleasantries, he cut to the chase and let me know that their children weren't interested in taking over the business and they would be keen to chat. We left it to the RACV commercial team to pick up the conversation, staying at arm's length to avoid any conflict of interest.

When the process was complete and we came up to meet some of their team, it was obvious they had the strong culture that we placed so much value on. Everyone seemed to love working together and there was a positive energy that washed over you when you entered the building. Tony was certainly a slick businessman, but I've had the same accusation levelled at me in the past, so I wasn't too concerned. I cheekily asked them what was with the ridiculous name Cola Solar, and whether they just picked it because it rhymes (it turned out that their family name was Cola). They also thanked me for agreeing to the RACV acquisition of Gippsland Solar, because they had gone out the next day and promoted themselves as 'the largest independent solar company in regional Victoria'.

It took a huge amount of effort to integrate Cola Solar into our business. With nearly forty employees, a large amount of infrastructure and dozens of contracts in various stages of delivery, it was a delicate process to manage, especially with the familiar campaign from jealous competitors trying to muddy the waters. We managed to complete the acquisition on time, keep the team together and secure all the contracts that were mid-flight.

Managing acquisitions is extremely hard work, and stressful at times, but it is immensely rewarding. It is an absolute privilege to identify great people that you can work with, and to be in a position to change their lives.

In the case of Tony and Kaye, there was one part of the story that I particularly loved. A few years earlier, they were forced to sell Kaye's family home to relieve some financial pressure. The house was sold, and at risk of being demolished for new townhouses. When we were well advanced in the acquisition discussions, Kaye was shocked to find that the house had come back on the market, and the sale of the business allowed her to buy it back and keep it in the family. When we all caught up to celebrate the acquisition, she told this powerful and heartfelt story, and she wasn't the only one to shed a few tears.

So much of the focus during acquisitions is on due diligence and analysing numbers. It's an important part of the process that you need to go through in detail, but for me, acquisitions are all about the *people*. You need to put yourself in the other person's shoes (and those of their team). Sometimes this means having honest conversations and being upfront with them about any potential impacts. When I was on the other side of the table in 2019, my biggest concern was reassuring my team and then having to go back on my word or looking foolish after the deal was done. When you bring empathy and honesty to the table, the result is much more beneficial for everyone involved.

By this stage, we had built a workforce of over 180 employees, and if you included contractors, that number bumped up to over 300. We had completed six acquisitions (including some smaller ones in the Gippsland Solar days), and we were piecing the jigsaw together successfully. Each acquisition provided a net-positive impact on our culture, ensuring that our employee engagement score was still at record highs.

But I sensed that moving at this pace was incredibly draining for my team. We were hustling like crazy to achieve RACV's growth mandate, at a time when the pandemic-related lockdowns had us scrambling to keep up with the latest ruling. Some of these restrictions were announced at 8pm and came into effect four hours later, meaning we had to contact dozens of customers and installers to cancel all projects for the following morning. We had to put down our tools for weeks (and sometimes months) when the Covid transmission rate started spiking, and the government brought in new restrictions. We had six lockdowns in Victoria, lasting 263 days and earning us the unwanted title of 'world's most locked down city'. We became familiar with phrases like 'stage 3 restrictions', which we used to associate with droughts and water usage. Then when restrictions were lifted or softened, we had to ramp up our installations overnight and play catch-up.

All of this had a major impact on the health and wellbeing of our team, and as someone who cared deeply for my people, this also took a huge personal toll on me. My own health was taking a battering again, and I was enduring many sleepless nights and recurring bouts of ulcerative colitis that confined me to bed. I would spend many of these days laid up at home with another flare-up, managing another crisis from my bed, with the phone ringing every few minutes and requiring my full attention. Kel was also working full-time, and with our primary school in lockdown, we were also trying to fulfil an additional role as teachers. Keeping the kids educated and entertained was incredibly draining, especially when the lockdowns prevented us from leaving the house for more than one hour per day.

The lockdowns finally relented in late 2021, but they were followed by economic shockwaves that had not been seen for many decades in Australia. The unprecedented impact on the economy, sagging business and consumer confidence, and a record ten consecutive interest rate rises placed the business under a different kind of pressure, but one that was no less stressful to navigate. The past few years had felt like being on the boxing ropes, copping a barrage of left and right hooks and trying to remain upright.

By working from home, I was able to keep up a veneer so my team didn't know much about my own struggles. But it was clearly unsustainable, and the business was moving faster and faster every day.

Kel and I lay in bed and had a deep discussion just before Christmas in 2022, after another sleepless night. As always, she cut through the waffle and hit the nail on the head. 'Look at you. You're not happy, and we're not living life the way we had intended.'

Kel made me an offer: if I stood down at the conclusion of my RACV contract at the beginning of June, she would take six months' leave from her job too. We would also step down from our coaching, umpiring and volunteer roles, and take some time to step off the hamster wheel and live life on our own terms. It was the hardest stage of life to clear the decks. We had just turned forty, had two jobs (and numerous unpaid roles), three children, a house, a dog, eight chickens and a pile of life admin to juggle. But we had to start somewhere.

That night, I booked five one-way flights to Europe. The rest would have to fall into place.

Chapter 26

Exit Stage Left

I was very comfortable with the decision, but having to keep this from my team and maintain my positive energy was extremely challenging.

I asked my chair, Nicole, if we could grab some lunch and cut straight to the point: 'I'm sorry, Nic, but I can't do it anymore. It's time to step down and prioritise my family for a while.'

As someone who has travelled a lot with her family and worked abroad, Nicole was immediately supportive and encouraging. She could also see that the flame had been flickering a bit in my eyes, so she had expected this conversation to take place. Once I addressed the elephant in the room, we had a very enjoyable lunch, reflecting on the incredible things we had achieved together. I'm sure she would agree that we had our moments over the years, but I feel very fortunate to have had Nicole as my chair. Her wisdom and counsel saw me through some particularly low points along the way.

We thrashed out the finer points over the next few weeks, built a CEO succession plan and agreed on the timing of the announcements. It is always destabilising when a founder exits the business and we were acutely aware that we needed to manage the transition effectively. I wanted my notice period to be no more than five days: I would make the announcement, get around to say farewell to my team and then clear the way so the business could move forward quickly.

There were too many challenges to mention on our business journey, but having to lead the team when you have one foot out the door was probably the most difficult. It requires all your energy and focus to support a large team, engage your clients and suppliers, manage acquisition discussions, and generally promote the interests of the organisation. And I've always believed you have to be 'all in' to be a great leader.

Something shifted from the moment I realised that my time was coming to an end. Maintaining relationships across my team and within RACV required more effort. I found it hard to discuss business planning, knowing that I wouldn't be in the role to see the plans through. When things became challenging, it was easy to give myself an 'out'.

Kel and I sat down and had a chat about how we wanted to make the most of this sabbatical from the workforce. We mapped out a five-month trip through fifteen countries in Europe and the Middle East, picking off as many challenges as possible to give the children the full travelling experience. None of these were English-speaking countries, except Ireland (which is still questionable!), so it was going to be an adventure to say the least.

Having been to over seventy countries ourselves, we wanted our three boys to share in the joy of exploring new places, and to experience the soaring highs and crashing lows that life on the road can throw at you. We never had that chance when the business sale went through, as we went headfirst into bushfires, a pandemic, lockdowns and travel restrictions. Our boys were now twelve, ten and eight, which is a great age for travel. No more nappies, they were all old enough to remember the trip, and our oldest boy, Lachie, was still very affectionate and yet to disappear into the combative and narcissistic teenage years (or so we'd been warned).

After my lunch with Nicole, I had my first decent night of sleep in months. I didn't have the slightest hesitation about whether I had made the right call. But in the week leading up to the announcement, I was overwhelmed by a sense of nostalgia. I wondered if I would ever have the same feeling of satisfaction and purpose again.

The day of the announcement was a blur. I addressed my team in a town hall meeting, spending some time reflecting on what the organisation had meant to me and how proud I was of each of them. Seeing the looks on their faces made me feel deeply emotional and made me realise how much I would miss working with them. I thanked them for their professionalism and friendship, closed my laptop and sat silently for twenty minutes as waves of emotion washed over me. It was done.

I hadn't expected it, but the feeling I had after announcing my resignation was even better than when we announced the acquisition.

It took me some time to land on a word for how I was feeling, but it became clear a few days later.

The feeling was satisfaction.

This satisfaction was vastly different to anything I had experienced in the past. Any sense of satisfaction along the way (even during the acquisition itself) was fleeting in nature. I had never stopped to smell the roses and enjoy success; it was always about moving on to the next challenge. But when I announced that I was standing down, it was like finishing the last chapter and closing the book.

The following week was an absolute whirlwind. I covered thousands of kilometres by plane, car and taxi, getting around to each of our locations to say thanks and farewell. I even managed a trip up to a conference in Sydney to spend some time with my team who were in attendance that week. It was a week full of laughs, hugs, a few tears and some incredible stories of the journey we had been on together. I received messages, phone calls and handwritten letters from the team, expressing what our relationship had meant to them.

The most moving letter was from Mitch, the charismatic young guy who I had developed through the business, and who had risen through the ranks to a senior leadership position. He said that apart from valuing our friendship immensely, what he appreciated the most was that he felt that we were invincible under my leadership. He always believed that we could achieve anything and that absolutely nothing was beyond us.

For a founder who has gone through an acquisition, the hardest part is knowing when it's time to go. You are so invested in what you have built, which can mean you end up staying for too long. Sometimes the relationship goes sour, you lose your passion or the ability to lead your team effectively, or you fail to realise that they might need a new voice. Even when things are going well, it's hard to know when you need a new challenge in your own life, or when it's time to shift your priorities. Money and power are incredibly addictive, and unless you thoroughly enjoy what you do, you can get stuck on the hamster wheel for far too long. Essentially, it's knowing when to leave at the 'top of the bell curve'.

It was time to hand over the baton, and move on to the next stage of our lives.

Chapter 27

One Door Closes …

As I write this chapter, we are halfway through our six-month break from the workforce, and 18,000 kilometres away from home.

I am spending every day embarking on adventures with Kelly and the boys, helping them with their schoolwork and creating memories that will last a lifetime. Of course, they are also driving us crazy at regular intervals. We are travelling in a motorhome, and by air, road, rail and sea across Europe and the Middle East. And much to the delight of Kel, we are enjoying the second of three consecutive summers. We've ticked off a bunch of sporting bucket list items: the Ashes, the Tour de France, the Running of the Bulls, Palio in Tuscany and the Italian F1 Grand Prix at Monza. Although I came off my mountain bike at great speed in the French Alps while trying to keep up with the kids (breaking my collarbone, dislocating my shoulder and tearing some ligaments), we are thoroughly enjoying every moment of the trip. And apart from taking time to write this book while my kids swim in the pool, I am resisting the temptation to interrupt my sabbatical.

I am sleeping as well as I have in a very long time, and my ulcerative colitis hasn't reared its ugly head since we left. After spending so much time ruminating on the decision to step down, it now feels like such an obvious thing to do.

This is not a 'happily ever after' story, as I'm sure there will be many more challenges in store for us. But it's a reminder that sometimes we need to take a deep breath and enjoy our time on this planet, rediscovering the things that bring us joy in life. Somewhere along the way on our business journey, I lost sight of what I truly value in life. The pressure of building our business and the desire to change the world became all-consuming and impacted heavily on my quality of life.

There's a big difference between those who enjoy winning and being successful and those who are obsessed by it. When you're obsessed, there is often a heavy price to pay. And for many years, I was prepared to pay that price.

But it wasn't just me who was paying the price. I was neglecting my most important role: that of a father and husband. I stopped kicking the footy, building sandcastles and reading bedtime books. When Kel was telling me about her day, I was subconsciously waiting for my chance to unload my daily stresses on to her. When my children showed me something they had been working on at school, I was physically present but energetically absent. I would find myself staring off into space for long periods and I'm certain that this energy rubbed off on them. At times, I was completely self-involved and not much fun to be around.

But for all the collateral damage that I suffered along the way, I am immensely proud of what we have achieved. We built a makeshift office in our garage, started a renewable energy business in coal country, gave up for a while, then doubled down and built it up to become one of the largest businesses of its kind in Australia. Across thirteen years, we created something from nothing, installed around half a million solar panels and thousands of batteries, and influenced many significant government policies and industry standards. We advocated heavily for increased safety and compliance in the industry, ensuring that our people (and those who work for our competitors) come home safely in the fulfilment of this renewable energy transition.

We employed some of the first female apprentices in the solar industry. And when we told their stories through our own channels and in partnership with the Clean Energy Council, we were inundated with interest from more women who saw installing renewable energy as a rewarding career path. We also took a leadership position on apprenticeships for Indigenous Australians, buoyed by the amazing journey that Orson came on with us. With Orson's blessing, we then created a mentoring program to attract more First Nations people into the renewable energy industry.

Across regional Victoria, we donated dozens of solar and battery systems to help treat injured wildlife, ensure reliable electricity for remote radio stations, educate students on the benefits of the energy transition and create safe meeting places for vulnerable communities. Some of those systems have subsequently been used to bring the community together during emergencies, providing some peace of mind during their most challenging times.

And I feel very strongly that we did all this without compromising our values. Every business needs to be financially sustainable so it can continue to exist, but we always believed that our primary objective was to do the right thing by people. If you set those core values and employ a team that lives and breathes those same values, you will enjoy business success as a result. The business is now in terrific hands and I can lay my head on the pillow every night knowing that the values we set for Gippsland Solar will continue to be upheld under RACV's ownership.

One of the most satisfying parts of the acquisition is reflecting on the opportunities it has created for our team. Gippsland Solar and RACV Solar have created opportunities for many hundreds of amazing people, and whether they have remained with the business, moved to another company or gone out on their own, I hope that they will make a big impact within the energy transition.

Remember Vince, the heavily mortgaged salesperson who took a leap of faith and embarked on a mature-age apprenticeship? He was nominated for the RACV Apprentice of the Year, selected from a huge pool of apprentices across the entire organisation. Vince went on to win the award at the RACV Gala Dinner, and his words of gratitude that night will stay with me forever.

I have been very fortunate to have amazing mentors, advocates and supporters in my own business life. There are so many of them that it would fill another book, and it's important to never forget the people who have helped you to become who you are. Especially in the early days when you had no influence or prospect of success.

It's Warwick, my mentor from the early days, who was never too busy to take a call with a silly question, and thrived on building my knowledge and experience.

It's Booma and Carmelo from the engineering company, who let me store my solar panels in their warehouse when I couldn't afford a forklift.

It's Damien, the electrician who spent thousands of dollars to obtain his solar accreditation in good faith, when I didn't have any work for him.

It's Latrobe City Council, which saw our potential and selected us for the business mentoring program, which introduced me to my business coach, Leigh.

It's our well-connected customers Aaron and Alana, who bought a system off me in 2011. After the roof leaked and caused thousands of dollars in plaster damage, Aaron rang me very calmly and said that no one would know about this if I took responsibility and fixed the damage. When we fixed everything up as promised and brought him a bottle of wine to apologise, he went on to become one of our strongest advocates, creating dozens of jobs for us.

It's Lew Fisher, the business leader from the Latrobe Valley who saw a younger version of himself in me. He not only gave us a 100kW contract but also took me under his wing, becoming one of my greatest (and toughest) mentors.

I sit here today at forty-one years old, hopefully halfway through my professional life. For all the support I have enjoyed as I built my career, I feel a strong sense of duty to pay it forward and support the next generation of entrepreneurs and renewable energy warriors. I have fostered hundreds of informal mentoring relationships with budding business owners over the past thirteen years, and always try to make time for them.

When a young Jake Warner from Penrith reached out to me in 2018, he said that he had followed my journey all the way through and wanted to build his own version of Gippsland Solar. He drove eleven hours each way to visit our new facility, mapped the whole warehouse out, went home and built a replica in his own factory. He was a sponge for knowledge. We have stayed close ever since that day and I have watched with great admiration as Jake has become an absolute industry powerhouse, building one of the most successful renewable energy businesses in the country. He messaged me when I announced my resignation, thanking me for years of mentoring, and saying how proud he was to have followed in my footsteps and then gone on to 'absolutely smoke everything we've achieved'. He's probably right!

While I don't know what's on my professional horizon, I know that it will leverage everything I've learned on my own journey. My strongest passions are mentoring, supporting start-ups and entrepreneurs, assisting governments and regulators to develop sensible and effective policies, and building blue-collar capability to accelerate the energy transition. We are well short of developing the workforce we need to achieve our net-zero targets, and some of the policies and barriers being implemented are only sending us backwards.

I'm not sure if I would ever start my own business again or take on another CEO role. As I sit here today, even the thought of it is exhausting, but time will tell. I've met a lot of CEOs and leaders along the way, and I remain convinced that leading with empathy and caring for your people is the recipe for success. I've found myself trying to change who I am over the years, and it has never worked for me. I will always be the type of leader who is not afraid to have a laugh or a hug, shed a tear or hit the dance floor with his team. I strongly believe that culture is the driver of all business success or failure, and a strong culture is far more important than sound strategy or financial capability.

Although I was always obsessed with business, I never wanted to be a serial entrepreneur, who spends their whole life building one thing after another. I wanted to prove I could do it, but I didn't want to lead a two-dimensional life where everything else was sacrificed for business success.

I always remembered something that one of my good friends, Claire, told me over a glass of wine a long time ago. She was talking about her passion for life and how she wished she could live four different lives at once. One life would be lived in nature, growing produce in the hills and living off the land in a simple and fulfilling way. One life would be lived travelling the world, with a mission to see every country in the world before she died. Another life would be lived raising a horde of children, creating life and giving them the guidance and empathy to become outstanding human beings. And the last life would be lived building a remarkable career, making a huge impact on the world through her professional endeavours. The value of this outlook always stayed with me; it's the very essence that life is short, and you have to live every single day as if it were your last.

I see life in phases. There was the phase when I met Kel and, having never had a passport before, spent the best part of five years travelling the world, taking risks, whittling our bank accounts down to zero on multiple occasions and experiencing everything the world had to offer. Then there was the foundational phase, where we knuckled down in Melbourne, worked long hours to build our careers and saved every cent we could to get ahead on our mortgage. The next phase was the tree change: moving our lives to a tiny town in the hills of Gippsland, starting a family and a business, volunteering for different groups and immersing ourselves in the community. It became our home in every sense of the word and allowed us to put down roots as a family, which our three boys will forever benefit from. The last phase was the exit from Gippsland Solar, handing over the business, which almost felt like my first-born child, and freeing us up to take a break from the workforce, and from life in general. We feel incredibly fortunate to be able to do this in our early forties, at the perfect time when we are physically capable, and the kids are old enough to remember the amazing times that we are sharing as a family.

So what does the next phase look like?

I have no idea, and that's a little unsettling. But I'm trying to live every day in the present moment and trusting that something will present itself when the time is right. Whatever happens, I feel like we have lived the way that Claire explained it. To grab every opportunity, remain in control of our own destiny despite the perceived external pressures, and to prioritise the things that bring us joy or fulfilment. What that looks like is different for everyone, but for us, it's about doing a bit of everything.

We are opening our children's eyes to what the world has to offer. I hope that this experience will encourage them to live their lives to the full. The world is full of joy and wonder, just waiting to be discovered.

Epilogue

Our Energy Future

Having closed the book on this chapter of our lives, I have had more time to reflect on the progress we have made as an industry, and the significant challenges that are yet to be addressed.

It's clear that when it comes to successful energy transition, the job is far from done. Especially for the Latrobe Valley.

While I try to maintain a positive outlook wherever I can, it's impossible to ignore the huge opportunity that Australia has missed within the energy transition.

We are a global leader in solar power. With over 30 per cent of homes (3.5 million systems) installing solar, we are ranked number 1 in the world per capita. There are around 2000 solar companies registered in Australia, and nearly 10,000 accredited installers. Despite a lack of consistent government policy regarding renewable energy from 2007 to 2020, Australian homes and businesses have just got on with it.

As the price of solar panels has fallen, rebates and incentives have been wound back accordingly, ensuring that the payback time for a solar system has usually hovered between four and seven years. The system has largely worked as it was intended.

We are now at the point where solar power is contributing anywhere between 50 per cent and 100 per cent of Australia's electricity needs at certain times of the day. It's a staggering number considering how quickly we have achieved it, and the rest of the world looks to Australia as a shining example of what is possible.

But we are also missing so much of the low-hanging fruit from this transformation. Over 80 per cent of the world's solar panels are made in China, and I can't see that changing any time soon. The saddest part for Australia is that almost every solar panel manufacturer in China learned their craft at UNSW, before being incentivised to move their business offshore and set up a manufacturing plant. It has been a tremendous outcome for consumers, with the price of solar panels falling by 500 per cent just in the period from 2010 to 2020. But at what cost to us in the long term?

There are already around 30,000 jobs in renewable energy in Australia. That number will increase many times over as we strive for our renewable energy targets, but we are still missing some vital parts of the vertical that could easily be captured within our shores. As I mentioned earlier, there was almost no importing of solar panels in 2001. Almost everything we installed was made right here in Australia, so I find it incredibly sad that we have let this opportunity slip. The great irony is that manufacturing solar panels uses a lot of electricity, and Australia has some of the lowest-cost electricity in the world during daylight hours. We could be leveraging this competitive advantage to bring more manufacturing back home.

While it's true that many jobs on the assembly lines have been replaced by robots and technology, there is a vast array of connected roles that would create many thousands of jobs as a direct result. Office administration, warehousing, transportation, finance, the list goes on.

We are making the same mistakes when it comes to battery storage for homes and electric vehicles. This trend is even more concerning, as we have some of the world's largest and highest-quality deposits of lithium (in the form of spodumene) in Western Australia. That raw material is shipped overseas, used to make lithium battery packs and then shipped back here. Again, around 80 per cent of the world's lithium batteries are currently made in China.

Like most of the big issues in the world, it is much easier to identify the problems than the solutions. So let's state what we know with reasonable certainty.

We know that the world is transitioning to renewable energy. Almost all our major trading partners have a net-zero target, and if we don't get serious about this transition ourselves, we will miss out on many billions of dollars in global trade. Anyone who says we shouldn't continue with the energy transition for economic reasons is not thinking holistically about it.

Within twenty-five years, we know, the existing coal-fired power stations will close. Barring some kind of bizarre and regressive policy backflip, we won't be building any more of them. That means we will lose over 15GW (15 million kW) of electricity generation in a very short period, which is nearly half of our entire supply. I happen to think they will stay open for much longer than some others have stated, due to the unacceptably slow rate that we are delivering renewable energy projects, but discussing that issue would take up a whole chapter by itself!

We know that Australia has currently installed over 35GW (35 million kW) of solar. There is enough usable area in Australia to install around 180GW, which would produce more electricity than what we currently consume per year. And that's just on the rooftops, without factoring in opportunities on the land.

With solar and wind replacing traditional generation, the profile of the entire electricity grid will change as a result. For the past few decades, we have had a large amount of excess supply overnight, because you can't just turn a power station up and down. This is why we designed off-peak tariffs, to encourage consumers to heat their water and their homes (with slab heating, for example) for only a few cents per kWh overnight. That approach was very effective when we had so much 'base load' supply, but it is no longer fit for purpose.

Solar electricity now provides up to 50, 60, and reaching 100 per cent of our needs, but only at certain times during the day. Before long, we will have far more supply than we need during the afternoon. It's a similar problem to what we faced in the past, but essentially 2pm is the new 2am.

To manage this transition effectively, we need to encourage people to use less electricity overnight. This is relatively simple for water heating: we can install heat pumps (which work most effectively during the afternoon) or smart hot water diverters (which use excess solar to run the electric element). Solving this issue alone will shift millions of kWh of electricity usage from overnight to daytime. And so long as everyone has enough hot water whenever they need it, they won't be affected in any way.

We should be turning some of our remote towns into microgrids. The RACV Solar team has already delivered some groundbreaking projects in this space, but there is much more to be done. Start with the most isolated and vulnerable communities, and reduce their reliance on the grid with solar, battery storage and smart hot water. Even backup generators would make more sense than our current system, which forces the electricity distributors to provide mains electricity to every home. This would save us from running long transmission lines through dense bushland, saving many millions of dollars in grid infrastructure and insurance. Everyone wins.

We should also be making consumers as self-sufficient as possible. By installing solar and battery storage on homes, businesses and community buildings (where the electricity is being consumed), we can greatly reduce their demand on the grid and ease the pressure on the rest of the network. It would defer a great deal of investment in new transmission lines and grid infrastructure. When combined with community batteries and energy efficiency improvements in homes and businesses, the benefits start to multiply greatly.

Electric vehicles are a much more complex issue. Despite all the latest developments in EV smart charging, the reality is simple. Nothing will ever be more convenient than charging your car while you sleep. Unless we can convince society to work all night and sleep all day, we must think outside the square to solve this issue.

Like so many of the issues, EVs can be seen as part of the problem or part of the solution. When you start to think of them as massive batteries on wheels, and solar panels as the petrol station, you begin to see the incredible opportunity that is in front of us. Remember that we will soon have far more electricity than we need during the day, meaning that electricity prices could be (and sometimes already are) in the negative. We might start charging our car during the day (perhaps at work), using that stored energy to run our home at night. Maybe we won't own the car – it might be leased to us by an energy company, and they will use these mobile batteries to create revenue streams that they can share with us through our electricity bill. Charging pillars for EVs will start popping up next to car parks, much like the old parking meters. Whenever an electric vehicle is stationary during sunlight hours, it will make economic sense to charge it. At night it will be the same, but it will instead be discharging into the grid and creating revenue for the vehicle owner.

By generating more solar electricity than we need during the day, we can also overcome one of the biggest challenges: how to ensure that *everyone* benefits from the shift to renewable energy. The sad truth about the transition so far is that it has widened the gap between those who are financially comfortable and those who aren't. It's fine if you own your home and have available space for solar panels and batteries, but what if you rent your home or live in an apartment? Those people have been left behind by the energy transition, and their bills have undeniably risen as a result of these incentives to others. But when we are awash with renewable energy in the grid, everyone can benefit from cheaper electricity during the day, even if it isn't installed on their own roof.

So what does this all mean for the Latrobe Valley?

In a word: opportunity.

The energy transition will mean that many hundreds of local jobs are at risk over the next twenty years. At the same time, we know that in order to meet our net-zero targets, we will need over 100,000 new workers in the renewable energy industry over the same time horizon. Those new job opportunities are incredibly diverse: semi and highly skilled, white and blue collar, and suitable for all ages and abilities. We need factory workers, apprentices, engineers, data scientists, administration assistants, finance experts, sales consultants, managers and directors. Many of these jobs could be created in coal heartlands like the Latrobe Valley, taking advantage of the infrastructure that has been set up to distribute electricity around the grid.

We should start by supporting power station workers with retraining, and thinking about which jobs are the most easily transferable given their relevant skillset. For many of them, there is a natural pathway from one field of electricity generation to another. If we were to offer free training or support for anyone who is interested in transitioning to the renewable energy sector, we could create far more jobs than those that are currently at risk. It's not easy, and that scares people. But it's entirely possible. And the one thing I am sure of is that the Latrobe Valley is ready.

Back in the early 2010s, some homeowners and businesses were actually afraid of showing their support for renewables. I had business owners ask me if we could install the solar panels 'around the back' (where the sun doesn't shine!) because they didn't want their customers to see them. But with each passing year, the community attitude towards renewables has started to turn. People have not only begun to see that the shift is inevitable but also that the region could benefit greatly from embracing it.

We have installed solar systems for hundreds of people who work in the coal-fired power industry. The reason they are doing it? Because it makes sense. Our largest ever system was installed in 2019, on the Latrobe Regional Hospital in Traralgon. Ten years earlier, it would have defied belief that we would be delivering a multi-million-dollar solar project in the heart of the valley, employing dozens of local workers for many months. But unlike in previous years, when some businesses felt that installing solar was a shameful secret, the hospital promoted this project widely and there was no community backlash.

When we started Gippsland Solar, only 2 per cent of homes in the Traralgon postcode had a rooftop solar system. In 2024, it sits at 27 per cent. And in my hometown of Mirboo North, it has leaped from 6 per cent to 39 per cent. Companies like Gippsland Solar are popping up everywhere, and installing solar is seen as a practical and common-sense move, without fear of reprisal from the community.

The inaugural Gippsland New Energy Conference was held in the

Latrobe Valley in 2022, and was completely sold out for both days, with over 500 attendees and seventy speakers. In the early 2010s, I felt like an alien at times, with few others to share my passion for the energy transition with. To think that, ten years later, we would be hosting the largest renewable energy conference in regional Australia is quite astounding. It is perhaps the greatest indicator of the incredible progress we have made. The work of Darren McCubbin and the Gippsland Climate Change Network (who organised the conference) has made a tremendous impact on our region, and this movement now feels unstoppable.

To continue this momentum, I am thrilled to announce that Kelly and I are establishing the Gippsland New Energy Scholarship to identify and nurture the next generation of renewable energy leaders. Through our foundation, we aim to support dozens of aspiring leaders – starting with those in the Latrobe Valley and Gippsland – to achieve their renewable energy ambitions. We will contribute a percentage from the sale of every copy of this book into the fund, and we have also secured a commitment from industry leaders to match our contribution. We will provide scholarship holders with access to industry events, conferences, networking opportunities, and training and accreditation, which will be relevant to their chosen career pathway. I will also connect them with my professional network and mentor them as they develop as leaders in their own right.

Stay tuned to my social media channels and LinkedIn feed for information on how to apply or nominate someone you know.

I can't wait to see where this transition to net-zero takes us. The past twenty-plus years have been an incredible ride, providing me and my team with experiences and opportunities we could only have dreamed of. But I have a strong feeling that, for the energy transition, and for the Latrobe Valley in particular, our best days are ahead of us.

If we can get it right, the future looks bathed in sunshine.